IN THE KILL ZONE

IN THE
KILL
ZONE

Surviving as a Private Military Contractor In Iraq

By Neil Reynolds

DELTA PUBLISHERS
JOHANNESBURG & CAPE TOWN

All rights reserved.
No part of this publication may be reproduced or transmitted, in any form or by any means, without the prior written permission of the publisher or copyright holder.

Copyright © Neil Reynolds 2018
Published edition 2018 © Jonathan Ball Publishers
Cover photo © John Moore/Associated Press
Back cover image is of author
Photos in the book © Neil Reynolds, except p 24 (Habiermalik/WikimediaCommons, p 73 (Jim Gordon/WikimediaCommons) and p 141 (Eric Powell/WikimediaCommons)

Published in South Africa in 2018 by
DELTA BOOKS
A division of Jonathan Ball Publishers
A division of Media24 (Pty) Ltd
PO Box 33977
Jeppestown
2043

ISBN 978-1-86842-856-4
ebook ISBN 978-1-86842-857-1

Every effort has been made to trace the copyright holders and to obtain their permission for the use of copyright material. The publishers apologise for any errors or omissions and would be grateful to be notified of any corrections that should be incorporated in future editions of this book.

Twitter: https://twitter.com/DeltaBooksSA
Facebook: https://www.facebook.com/DeltaBooksSA/
Blog: http://jonathanball.bookslive.co.za/

Cover by Johan Koortzen
Design and typesetting by Martine Barker
Editing by Mike Nicol
Proofreading by Alfred le Maitre
Set in Gill Sans/Baskerville

Printed by **novus print**, a Novus Holdings company

This book is dedicated to all who worked with me in Iraq: Rieme de Jager; Eddie Visser; Snoeks Niewhoud; Gerhard Nel; Mauritz le Roux; John Walbridge; and many others.

CONTENTS

The Baghdad Four
1

1. 'Want to work in Iraq?'
3

2. Destination, Middle East
9

3. Gearing up
19

4. Reconnoitring Baghdad
37

5. The Sunni triangle of death
54

6. Setting up the company
60

7. The contracting business
69

8. A day in the Green Zone
81

9. The Kuwait misadventure
91

10. Down to business
96

11. The scrap metal convoy
107

12. First major contract
114
13. The best-laid plans
131
14. The battle of Fallujah
139
15. Near misses
142
16. Villa T-Bone
150
17. Ordinary deaths and cloak-and-dagger work
158
18. Expansion and new contracts
165
19. In the kill zone
178
20. Two deadly ambushes
189
21. Making a plan in Dubai
203
22. Going high-profile
217
23. The Baghdad Four continued
228
24. The end of OSSI/Safenet
235
Postscript
244

The Baghdad Four

Iraq, Baghdad. Many times I have imagined this scene. Many times I have played it out in my mind.

It was Sunday, 10 December 2006. I had been in Iraq for three years working in the private military security industry.

On that day we sent a convoy to Kirkush in the northeast of the country, about 200 km from Baghdad. Up front in this convoy was a Nissan sedan, followed by a GMC armoured vehicle, followed by a Kia 12-seater minibus, which acted as the gunship (CAT, counter-assault team) to repel any attack on the convoy by insurgents.

It was a particularly tense mission. There had been a couple of attempts to truck our client's material to Kirkush but these had all fallen foul of insurgent activity. The equipment was critical to a construction project and this mission had to succeed.

We had four expat members of our staff and five Iraqis as the security detail running the mission. The expats were South Africans: André Durant (38), Johann Enslin (48), Callie Scheepers (48) and Hardus Greeff (43). All were experienced, all were men who could be relied on in a difficult situation. But, experience aside, they would have been tense and alert from the moment they left the relative security of the Dohra power station, one of our compounds, for Kirkush.

On the outskirts of Baghdad, the convoy arrived at one of the many checkpoints in and around the city and came to a halt. This is where my imagination takes over, where I keep replaying the scene.

The Iraqis manning the checkpoint were most probably wearing uniforms of the Iraqi police or army. There was no way for the team to know it was a fake checkpoint set up by insurgents. I was later told one of the Iraqis asked them to evacuate the vehicles for an inspection.

This was an unusual procedure, but I can imagine that André, as the team leader, did not want to aggravate a situation that was volatile by its nature, so the men complied.

'Make your weapons safe!' came the next instruction.

Again the men complied.

'Hand over your weapons for the inspection. Also you will not need to wear your body armour. Take it off.'

I can imagine that at this point André protested. I can imagine that guns were pointed at them, that they tried to defuse the situation. But it escalated quickly.

'You will come with us. Move, move, move.'

And, being prodded by the barrels of AK-47s, they would have been forced into vehicles and taken away.

They were all family men. They had wives. They had children. They would become known as the Baghdad Four.

They are part of my story.

1
'Want to work in Iraq?'

In early July 2003 I was living in the small town of Mtunzini on the KwaZulu-Natal north coast. My wife, Vivienne, and I had bought there in the late 1990s while I was still in the South African National Defence Force (SANDF) and second in command of Group 27, a commando unit that was based in Eshowe and had since been phased out.

For the previous three years I had worked in northern Angola as in-house security for the diamond mining company International Trading and Mining. My mission was the safekeeping of the diamonds during the mining process, from extraction to sorting. However, in 2003 I decided for personal reasons not to renew my contract.

I hadn't been home a week before Mauritz le Roux, the owner of Safenet Security, phoned. I had worked for Safenet before my stint in Angola and had kept in touch with Mauritz. Now Mauritz was on the phone as if we talked weekly.

'I heard you'd left Angola,' he said. 'Want to work in Iraq?'

Iraq? I had no idea where Iraq was and only a vague idea that a war was raging there from watching BBC News when I was still on the mine. Minor details.

'Ja, of course,' I responded. 'When do we leave?'

'I want you to meet my partner before we settle on a contract. He's an American, named John Walbridge. Can you get up to Pretoria for a meeting?'

'No problem. I'll catch an early flight tomorrow.'

Leaving home at the drop of a hat seemed to have become

a common thing with me, and my family had got used to this coming and going. Truth be told, I suspect my presence upset their routine, as they were accustomed to living without me. Too much of Dad was not necessarily a good thing.

Fortunately, Vivienne is a very understanding wife, and when I told her I was going to Pretoria for a few days to explore a job option she was supportive. I mentioned that it would be an overseas contract but didn't mention Iraq. More than that I couldn't say, as more than that I didn't know. I packed an overnight bag with my trusty jeans and T-shirts and wore smart casuals and a jacket for the meeting. The next morning I was on the first flight out of Durban.

I am a military man through and through. In 1980 I was called up for my two-year national service at the Infantry School in Oudtshoorn. There I completed my junior leader's training. Eventually, I was posted to the operational area of South West Africa (today Namibia). After my first contact, I was hooked. I knew I wanted to be a professional soldier and decided to join the Permanent Force.

By November of that year I was in the reconnaissance wing of 31 Battalion at Omega in the Caprivi Strip. There I got to work with a group of Bushmen who taught me everything I needed to know about bush warfare. They were incredible.

After eight years in the Caprivi I was transferred back to South Africa and the Department of Foreign Affairs. My next posting was to the Venda Defence Force, until a military coup occurred in that homeland. The South African embassy in Venda felt that I had been too involved in the coup and advised that I leave the 'country'. I was posted to the Infantry School in Oudtshoorn and to various other positions until I took the early retirement package from the military at the end of 1999.

At that point I did some private security work for Mauritz le Roux's company Safenet for a few months. They had a contract to provide security for Tiger Brands when I joined them in 2000. My army buddy Gerhard Nel, with whom I had been deployed on a number of missions with 31 Battalion's recce wing, was the CEO of Safenet at the time and introduced me to Mauritz.

The work for Safenet was occasional and by June 2001 I took a longer-term contract in northern Angola at the diamond mining company. This was my first taste of the commercial security industry. The contract conditions were six months on the mine followed by a month's leave. Being out there in the bush meant almost total isolation. There was no internet. We were allowed a five-minute phone call home once a week using the satellite phone. It was tough on our families, and not easy for us either.

From time to time we escorted the diamonds from Lucapa to Luanda for a diamond sale, but other than those occasions our world was limited to the mine. Fortunately the food was good. As was the remuneration. I earned more in a month than I had in a year in the army. And there was a bonus of 50% of your salary if the mine extracted diamonds in excess of 25 000 thousand carats in a month.

I had some amazing times on the mine and I learnt a few things that would come in very handy in the months and years to come. For one, I learnt my way around international airports. At the time, most of the military guys were not very experienced travellers – boarding a C-160 at Waterkloof Air Force Base was a big thing. This had also been the limit of my flying experience. Not once in my 20-year military career had I flown on a commercial plane.

While working on the mine was lucrative, I decided not to renew my contract in 2003 because I wasn't sure that either my family or I could last another bout. That meant I was open to exploring other opportunities and the reason why I didn't think twice about flying to Pretoria to meet with Mauritz.

Later that day, at Mauritz's Waterkloof Ridge house, he introduced me to John Walbridge. John was the son of an American army veteran and had grown up on bases in Hawaii, Germany and New Jersey. His training had been at the Citadel, an elite military college in South Carolina. After graduating in 1969, he'd joined the 5th Special Forces Group. From the army he moved to the CIA and saw deployments in Africa, Europe and Latin America. In Africa, in what was then Rhodesia (today Zimbabwe), he'd met a South African woman and they'd married. Since 1995 he'd been retired, if running a commercial security firm could be called retirement.

Mauritz's background was equally colourful. He'd been a lieutenant in the Engineer Formation in the South African Defence Force (SADF) and been involved with the rebel movement, UNITA, in operations in and around the town of Jamba in southern Angola.

When Executive Outcomes – a private military company formed by soldiers disbanded from various battalions in the SADF in the early 1990s – undertook its first operation at Soyo in northern Angola in 1993, Mauritz was among their number. Some years later he'd started Safenet and contracted security services to a number of Pretoria companies. He was also a director in a company called Stablico, which had links to the Mobutu Sese Seko government in then Zaire, now the Democratic Republic of Congo.

I could see why Mauritz liked John, as the man was approachable and relaxed and we clicked from the off.

He and Mauritz lived in the same gated estate in Pretoria. Their wives were friends and it was through their wives that they had met. Soon enough they were discussing Iraq and the potential it offered a good security provider. John already had a small contract to supply security personnel to a telecommunications company in Iraqi Kurdistan, a proto-state in the northeastern part of the country, but he was trying to expand his business. Their idea was to form a joint venture called OSSI/Safenet and put in a bid for a security contract for a telecommunications company in Kurdistan.

John had an ex-policeman, Casper Oosthuizen, working for him in the town of Sulaymaniyah in Kurdistan who was supposed to investigate new business opportunities for him. He had met Casper while looking for operators to assist him with providing security at the Olympic Games that were to be held in Greece in 2004. Casper claimed he had been part of a South African police task force but we were never sure about this. In Iraq he was recruiting locals and putting together the basic equipment that would be needed for a security operation.

Mauritz and John invited me to come over again the next day to meet the rest of the team they'd recruited and who would be heading for Iraq in an effort to secure the telecommunication bid. The rest of the team turned out to be ex-Recces (Special Forces operators): Rieme de Jager from 5 Reconnaissance Regiment; Snoeks Niewhoud from 4 Reconnaissance Regiment. Then there was Eddie Visser, a highly qualified medic with a bubbly personality and an ability to make friends with anybody. His personality would be a considerable asset to the team.

Both Rieme and Snoeks had been senior NCOs in the Special Forces and the three of us had an instant rapport. That Eddie didn't have a military background was of little concern, as it wasn't expected and he was clearly a team man.

The decision was made: we would head for Iraq with Mauritz just as soon as we could get all our paperwork in order.

2
Destination, Middle East

Some quick internet searches brought me up to speed on the topic of Iraq. On 20 March 2003, Iraq had been invaded by a multinational coalition led by the United States as part of what was called 'the war on terror'. This followed the attack on the World Trade Center in New York on 11 September 2001 by al Qaeda terrorists. The American government (incorrectly) believed Iraqi president Saddam Hussein had developed nuclear and biological weapons, and also that he supported al Qaeda.

Over the next 21 days the Coalition Forces captured the capital city, Baghdad, and deposed the Ba'athist government of Saddam Hussein. The Coalition Forces also received support from the Peshmerga, the armed forces of Iraqi Kurdistan.

The invasion would lead to a long period of insurgency that ranged from heavy weaponry battles in the deserts to firefights in the streets, suicide bombings, assassinations, mortar attacks, car bombs, hijackings and the introduction of roadside bombs, which would come to be responsible for most of our injuries as security personnel. Hussein, who went into hiding, was caught in December 2003. (He was eventually sentenced to death and hanged in 2006.)

While war raged in Iraq, we tried to figure out how to get there. Until my internet searches, I hadn't even known where it was on the map, so my first step was to do what in the army we called a 'map appreciation' to establish which countries bordered Iraq. Soon our research also showed that there were no direct flights to Iraq. In fact, there were no flights into Iraq, full stop. The closest routes were to Kuwait, Jordan and Turkey. Iran and Syria were not options.

Getting to Iraq wouldn't have been such an issue if we had secured a US government contract in advance. The only direct flights into Iraq were on US military transports, and private military contractors who worked on a US government contract were able to secure seats on these flights. You were also issued a DoD (Department of Defense) badge, which was useful if you needed to travel through Kuwait, as Kuwait did not issue visas to South Africans.

John had considerable experience of international travel. However, international travel on a US passport is a lot easier than travel on a South African one. I had discovered this in Angola when needing visas to enter that country, a process that was bureaucratically tiresome and took days.

As we broke down the options for getting to Iraq we realised we probably wouldn't qualify for Kuwaiti visas but that Jordan was one of the few countries South Africans did not need a visa to enter. Ideal for us. However, Americans needed a visa for Jordan, which was somewhat ironic.

The next issue was getting from Amman in Jordan to the Iraqi border. And would there be a functional border crossing between the two countries after the war that had raged there? On top of that, we would have had to travel the length of Iraq through the war zone to get to the northern area where we were planning to set up our services. Would we find vehicles capable of doing the journey? Was the journey even feasible?

'What about Turkey?' I suggested.

To get to Turkey meant flying to Milan, Italy, and connecting to Istanbul. From Istanbul we could take a domestic flight to the city of Diyarbakir in southeastern Turkey. A hire car and a six hour drive would get us from there to the Iraqi border. This was a long route but at least we knew there was a proper border crossing into northern Iraq.

Another advantage was that John had Casper Oosthuizen in Sulaymaniyah, in nearby Iraqi Kurdistan, who had on-the-ground experience and could set up accommodation. And, as a Turkish visa was a mere formality, that route was bedded down.

That evening I phoned Vivienne.

'The contract's in Iraq,' I told her somewhat hesitantly.

'Are you going to be safe?' The concern in her voice was touching and made me smile.

'Of course. Look, do me a favour will you, could you courier up my passport. I've got to get a visa.'

'Okay,' she said. 'But you're absolutely sure about this?'

'It's a great opportunity,' I reassured her.

Once the visa applications had been submitted it was a matter of waiting. We went our separate ways for the next three months until the documentation was cleared. Then things got hectic. Flight tickets were booked and Mauritz arranged $50 000 for operating expenses. We spent the days before departure planning what we would need to take with us, and what we would need in Iraq to operate as a private military security company. Deciding on the equipment was an issue in itself, as each guy had his own requirements and priorities. We soon realised Rieme was not going to accept anything less than what was on his list. He was not the kind of guy you argued with because you would not win.

Eddie sourced medical supplies that would be adequate for the worst possible scenarios, because we had no idea of the medical support there or if we would be able to use the US military's facilities. He also had a file documenting the medical equipment in case there were customs queries.

The heavy equipment came down to body armour, radios, helmets and weapon cleaning kits. It looked like we wanted to start a war. I realised we might have difficulty getting through customs and border controls in some of the countries.

The band of brothers departs from Johannesburg for Iraq. From left to right: Eddie Visser, me, Rieme de Jager and Snoeks Niewhoud.

Everything was packed into three tin trunks – specially made for the purpose thanks to a manufacturer Mauritz knew – with the more military items at the bottom so that a cursory border search would not arouse suspicions. We were dressed in civvies although we were wearing similar clothing. The closest we could risk getting to a uniform. Luckily we did not simply accept the wisdom that because there were deserts in Iraq it would always be hot regardless of the season. It was winter in Europe so we took proper winter jackets. Little did we know how much we would need them.

Passing through Johannesburg International Airport (today OR Tambo International Airport) wasn't easy. The trunks were heavy, their handles thin and difficult to grip for too long. We had to stop frequently to ease the cramp in our hands. I felt as if everyone was staring at us.

In fact, at any moment I expected the police to stop us and demand to know what was in the trunks. If this happened, our cover story was that we were medics on a mission to help with the crisis in northern Iraq. At the time there was serious fighting between the Kurds and the Turkish military on the Iraq border, so the story was feasible.

At the check-in counter we were questioned by a pretty young woman processing passengers, and the ever-charming Eddie rolled out our story. With the help of her supervisor, our trunks, plastered as they were with medical supplies stickers, were checked through to Istanbul, and I heaved a sigh of relief that we'd got through so easily. Although there was still the concern that the real test was still to come in Turkey.

However, customs had a little tense moment for us. An official asked to check Mauritz's rucksack and found the $50 000.

'I'm sorry,' the official said, 'you can only take out $20 000.'

'What?' demanded Mauritz. 'What do you mean?'

'That's the exchange control rules,' he was told.

Mauritz freaked. Waved his hands, went puce in the face.

'Then I'll tear up the rest of the notes.'

'Hey, hey, Mauritz,' I said, taking $30 000 from him and giving $10 000 to Eddie.

'That sorts it?' I asked the customs guy. 'We're all travelling together.'

He shrugged and waved us through.

Europe was in the grip of an icy winter and a cold front had blanketed the region in snow. Due to the weather conditions the flight from Milan to Istanbul was a bit bumpy, to say the least. I started to worry that we might not be able to land there and would be diverted to another country, which would've been a nightmare given our luggage.

Fortunately, we managed to land even if it took around 40 minutes. Istanbul was snowed in and the airport had snow-ploughs working constantly to clear the runways. The last time I had seen snow I was a mere boy, so the sight of the white landscapes was a novelty and beautiful.

Istanbul airport was chaos. Flight cancellations meant irritable passengers and long queues everywhere. My fears regarding the possible issues we could have with the kit immediately doubled. But then I had another thought.

'Maybe this is a good thing,' I said to Mauritz. 'All this mess could help us check the trunks through because the ground staff will be under a lot of pressure.'

To a degree I was right. When we arrived at the security counter at the domestic terminal, the officer nearly did a backflip at the sight of our three trunks. Of course he could not speak English, and ran off to find someone who could. It took a while for him to come back with a colleague who immediately asked what we had in the trunks. Eddie spun the story of our humanitarian mission, but the officer insisted that we pack out the trunks since they were too big to fit through the scanner.

Here we go, I thought. The end of our mission. But then Mauritz jumped in.

'No problem,' he said to the security officer, and started unpacking the trunk numbered 3 that we knew contained the medical equipment. We had a list of all the equipment in the trunk which he duly gave to the officer. He also presented Eddie, who had suddenly been promoted to a doctor. Soon there was quite a scene, with the equipment lying all over the place and people trying not to step on it. We had only packed out about half of the trunk when the officer told us to stop and waved us through.

Our connection was cancelled so we were faced with a possibly long wait. The terminal was crowded and all the seats taken so we had to sit on our trunks. Throughout the night we worked shifts to stay awake and look after the kit. We divided into buddy pairs as in the army. We had a two-man team and a three-man team. I hoped that we would be able to fly to Diyarbakir first thing in the morning.

I was soon faced with yet another challenge: I needed the toilet. I had expected the bathrooms to be very busy given all the stranded passengers, but they were mostly empty. Why? It was prayer time. I was slowly starting to learn something of the Muslim world.

However, when I stepped into the first cubicle there was no toilet, just a hole in the floor and a little hosepipe. Hell, I thought, they must be busy with maintenance.

I asked a local where the toilets were. He pointed at the cubicles. 'Arabic toilets,' he said in broken English. 'All fine.'

'No seats,' I said.

He then directed me to the business class lounge where he said there were Western toilets.

Had there been toilet paper I would have used the 'hole' toilets, but the little hosepipe put me off. Fortunately, given the flight cancellations, the business-class toilet was open to all. I decided there and then that I'd always keep a supply of 'white gold' in my pocket.

During the night I got into conversation with an old woman sitting near us. She spoke English and gave me useful information about our destination – she lived in the region – and about the border post between Iraq and Turkey. It seemed that this could be a challenge. The fighting in the area meant that the controls were rigorous. She also said it would be cold, since Sulaymaniyah was surrounded by mountains.

'Have all your papers in the right order,' she said. 'Otherwise you will sit for a very long time. Also take food and water.'

Another thing that amazed me at the airport was that people had plugged their cellphones in all over the place to charge and simply left them there. Nobody touched the phones. I asked the old woman about this and she explained that no one would steal your phone if it was busy charging. Coming from South Africa, I was gobsmacked by this.

The next morning, as a parting gift, she gave me a beanie she had been knitting throughout the night. 'You will need this for your head,' she said.

In the morning, when our flight was called, Rieme realised he had lost his air ticket. The only solution was for Mauritz to buy another one for him, which did not improve Mauritz's mood, by now tense and angry after the long and uncomfortable night. Luckily they accepted credit cards. What we didn't know was that this was the last place we could use our cards.

The flight to Diyarbakir was short. My big worry then was how we were going to get the trunks from the airport to the hotel and from there to the Iraqi border post. There was no way our trunks would fit into a sedan.

As we landed I noticed F-16 jets parked on the side of the runway and realised there must be an American base nearby that was flying missions into Iraq. This was possibly a good sign. At least some people might speak English. Fortunately we got through customs without any trouble and found taxis that could get us and the trunks to a hotel. All the while I was waiting for a policeman to come running over demanding that we open the trunks.

Once we stepped out of the terminal building, we were swamped by taxi drivers. They all wanted our business but we couldn't understand a word they said. Then one of them shouted to me in English and I called him over. It turned out he could easily arrange for four station wagons to take us and our luggage to the hotel and also drive us to the border post the following day and even onward to the first town of Zahko.

For the rest of that day we walked around Diyarbakir. I was surprised to see that shops selling similar items were all in the same street. I would later learn that this was also typical of other Muslim countries. All the mechanical shops were next to each other, then you'd find the clothing stores together, and so on.

The lovely smells emanating from a bakery soon drew our attention. Mauritz gave the baker $2 and for that we got ten flat breads of a kind I had never seen before. We washed it down with Turkish coffee served at a shop next door. The coffee was so strong your eyes almost popped out. Rieme loved it – the stronger the better for him. It also had sediment at the bottom, so you had to be careful not to drink that, too. I must admit, I preferred the tea.

3
Gearing up

The next morning the taxis arrived early, as we had arranged. The weather was bitterly cold and it was snowing. I was grateful for the old lady's beanie. We set out in convoy with Rieme and Snoeks in the first vehicle, Eddie and me in the second, and Mauritz in the third with the trunks. It was a six-hour drive to the border with one stop for coffee and to refuel. Close to the border there were long queues of trucks, mostly oil tankers, lining the road. These trucks worked a continual shift into Iraq to the oilfields to load the crude oil, which was then taken back to Turkey for refining.

It took two hours to be cleared through the Turkish customs where we had to complete a form to explain where we were going to, what we would be doing, where we would stay, etc. They seemed to take their time trying to confirm our story. Once cleared at customs, we had to go through a Turkish intelligence checkpoint. Only then could we drive across to the Iraqi border post where Casper and a Peshmerga team were waiting to take us to Sulaymaniyah.

At the intelligence checkpoint we were met by two uniformed officers and an intelligence guy. Again they wanted the whole story about our medical missions. The uniformed guys wanted to check the trunks and again we started unpacking trunk 3 with the medical equipment. After probing us about some of the items, the officials told Eddie and me (with trunk 3) that we could move on to the Iraq border post.

We left the other team members behind and drove the

Mauritz le Roux (right) and me having a coffee on the road between Diyarbakir in Turkey and the Iraqi border.

few hundred metres to the Iraqi border post. There the Iraqi custom officials were just about to stamp our passports when their telephone rang. They had what sounded like quite a serious conversation. When they were done, they gave our passports back and indicated that we had to go back to the Turkish border post.

What now, I wondered? When we got back to the rest of the team at the Turkish intelligence checkpoint, all the trunks had been packed out. Oh shit, I thought. The intelligence guy was agitated and grilled us about the equipment. Why body armour? Why helmets? Why radios?

We told him it was for our protection. There was a war on, after all. Eventually he accepted this explanation but the radios still bothered him. 'So that we can keep in contact,' I explained.

'You must have a letter from your embassy for the radios,' he insisted.

To this we did not have a solution.

'Without this letter you cannot cross the border.'

'Okay,' said Mauritz, 'I will go back for the letter. Can the other men go through?'

'Yes,' he said. 'Yes, that is all right.'

Just as we started repacking the trucks one of the officials found the weapon cleaning kits and took it to the intelligence agent. Immediately his attitude changed.

'What is this for?'

'For cleaning baby bottles,' Eddie explained. An ingenious and quick answer. With a lot of hand signals to clarify the intended purpose of the brushes, we convinced the officer that they were innocent items. Fortunately, there were only two kits.

'You can go through,' he said.

We packed those trunks as fast as we could. We wanted to get out of there before they changed their minds. I arranged to return in three days to collect Mauritz, who would be joined by John at that time.

'Here,' he said, giving me $10 000. 'Be careful with it.'

The taxis were loaded up and we drove across no-man's-land to the Iraqi border post. There our passports were stamped within two minutes and we were finally free to go. Casper and the Peshmerga team had come in four Land Cruisers and we loaded the kit. They were keen to be under way as we would only reach Sulaymaniyah late in the night.

With the snow it would not be an easy drive. We set off at an alarming speed which the drivers maintained with reckless abandon. They seemed to think the Land Cruisers were Formula 1 racing cars. I asked our driver whether he could go a little slower but he said he was following the lead vehicle and they determined the speed the convoy drove at.

I tried to relax, at least pleased that we had got this far with the kit, bar the hitch with the radios that I was convinced Mauritz would sort out. After the nightmare drive we arrived at a comfortable hotel where Casper had booked our accommodation.

The next morning I woke to see we were surrounded by mountains white with snow. As there was a little park near the hotel, I dressed warmly and went for a run to shake off the jet lag.

Later, after breakfast, we reccied the streets around the hotel. Given the everyday street life at the pavement cafes and takeaway joints selling chicken and lamb shawarmas (the aroma was enough to make your mouth water), and the flow of people, with the men in traditional dress and the women with scarves over their hair, it was easy to forget that this was a war zone. Easy to forget that a lot of people we walked past probably resented our presence.

In one street we came across shops that sold military equipment, and it seemed that we could buy anything we wanted. Not wishing to draw attention to ourselves, we returned to the hotel. Besides we were not armed and had no idea of the security situation in Sulaymaniyah.

An irritated Casper awaited us at the hotel. We should not have gone off without him, he said. It was dangerous.

His attitude riled Rieme, who disliked policemen at the best of times, and Casper had once been a cop. Perhaps because of his overbearing attitude he would never really be part of the team, and eventually he left the company.

But now he sat with us to explain the situation. His briefing described this part of Kurdistan as fairly quiet; we could move around safely. All the same, we would need to be street smart.

'It is best not to go out on your own,' he said.

We then decided to always go about in buddy pairs. This

made sense, as it was how we'd operated in the bush.

At this time in Iraq there was no cellphone network and we could not call each other if there was a problem. Also, the internet was limited – so, admittedly, was our knowledge of the internet, as we hadn't kept pace with technology. We came from an era when you navigated by maps and compass.

Fortunately I had my laptop, because I had been charged with keeping track of all our expenses. And anyway, after my time in Angola I had vowed that I would never go anywhere again without a laptop. If I had had one there, at least I could've contacted Vivienne via email. For the first few years in Iraq it was the only means of communication we had with family and anyone else for that matter. In fact, that laptop became the centre point of our business.

During our time in Iraq, communications technology would change radically. Cellphone networks would be built; there would be Skype, Google Earth, GPS devices. These advances would spill over into how the war was fought and be integrated into the military systems. The US military were hardly going to supply us with equipment but they required that a civilian contractor's equipment synced with their own.

For instance, the Track 24 vehicle tracking system – which was already in use in South Africa – was upgraded for use by the US military. The reason for the upgrade was that, once on contract, the US military tracked our every mission. They could notify us in advance of any problems on our route and they also supplied the medical evacuation and response team. In fact, they would approve the mission's route and any alternatives. Without this clearance, a mission would have been stopped at the first checkpoint.

Casper told us he had already bought two Nissan Patrols

second hand but in perfect condition with low mileage. We had seen other personal security detail (PSD) teams driving around in these vehicles, so they were clearly the vehicle of choice.

The armaments he had acquired included: four MP5s (a 9 mm sub-machine-gun of German design) and a PKM machine gun (a 7.62 mm general-purpose machine gun designed in the then Soviet Union and currently in production in most former Eastern Bloc countries, including China). While you didn't want to be defending yourself with a 9 mm against an AK-47, the MP5 was smaller and easier to handle in a vehicle than an AK. And the PKM more than made up in firepower what we lacked by not having AKs.

A PKM machine gun.

Casper also assured us he had bought a lot of ammunition. I did not ask where he had acquired these weapons but from what we'd seen in the street, they could be over-the-counter purchases or out of a car boot.

Despite Casper's briefing and our hardware, it must be said that none of us had any idea of personal security detail work. We were military guys. We knew about guns and military tactics. Personal security was a police task. However, the basic principles were the same, and common sense would supply the rest.

Casper, as he had been in the area for a while and had the backing of police experience, undertook to train us in personal security tactics. I could see this grated on Rieme but he went with it for the moment. I had my doubts that he'd take orders from a policeman – even a former policeman – indefinitely.

For the rest of that first day I accounted for Casper's expenses and compiled spreadsheets for easy reading. We were also able to dial up an internet connection and contact our families. I let Vivienne know that I had arrived and was safe and staying in a really nice hotel. We had both expected that we could be in touch by cellphone, so it was a disappointment having to make do with email and online messaging.

Apart from Casper's briefing, we also needed to understand our environment. One thing I had noticed was the absence of traffic. There were lots of trucks – they were the major means of transporting goods as there was no train service at this time – but hardly any cars. From locals at the hotel we learnt that no one had spare cash to buy cars, a situation that would change rapidly throughout 2004.

On the missions we would run to the Jordanian border towards the end of 2003, we'd see truckloads of second-hand vehicles being taken to Baghdad. Jordan and Turkey and Kuwait were quick to take advantage of the Americans' moving into Iraq. Turkey supplied fuel, as did Kuwait, which had allowed the Americans to set up a major base. Consequently, transport and catering businesses opened up in Kuwait to support the US mission.

As I've mentioned, Kurdistan is mountainous. Once, according to the locals, the mountains had been covered in forests but these were cut down on the orders of Saddam Hussein to prevent the Peshmerga from seeking refuge in the forests. In later years the UN would start a reforestation project. I was also told that Saddam's forces had killed a whole village using chemical warfare. I hadn't realised the extent of the antagonism between Kurdistan and Iraq, or that the Kurds and the Iraqis did not even speak the same language.

There were a lot of lessons learnt in those early days that would be a help in the future when the company moved to other countries. They also taught us what to research and what was critical to the success of a mission. With this background the company could go into a new country and be up and running almost immediately.

Soon enough, an email from John confirmed that he had met up with Mauritz and that they would be at the border the following day. This was an excellent opportunity for a training mission. Casper supplied weapons and we decided to send three vehicles: Casper in the rear, Rieme and Snoeks in the lead, followed by Eddie and me. On the return trip Mauritz would travel with us and John with Casper. It was important that we got into the swing of this new game as quickly as possible.

We had all the military skills necessary: what we lacked was the aggression of Iraqi drivers, an ease with driving on the right-hand side of the road, and proper navigation equipment. The only maps we had, the only maps available, were tourist maps. The only answer was to learn the road systems of the areas we were operating in as thoroughly as we could.

Local drivers weren't an option. As Rieme bluntly put it: our Peshmerga friends had learnt to drive on video games. So the mission to the border was an opportunity for route reconnaissance and training.

At ten to five the next morning we were stoked on coffee when the Iraqi team leader walked in dead on time. Great, at least they know about sticking to a schedule, I thought. But I was wrong to think this was typical of all Iraqi people. I was then not yet familiar with the expression 'inshallah', meaning 'God be willing'. It was a favourite expression that we South Africans would come to dread, since it went along with a seemingly laid-back attitude towards most events. The Iraqis believed it gave them permission to be late for everything, and it was also used when they told you what they thought you wanted to hear, which was not necessarily the truth.

By dawn we were on the road, the terrain hazy in the early light. One thing I soon realised was that the radio handsets the Peshmerga used didn't work unless the vehicles were bumper to bumper, and I was glad that Casper had spent the money on proper vehicle radios. In a contact situation we would need comms between the vehicles.

Our convoy of three vehicles drove in a specific order. First there was the lead vehicle, and then the second vehicle, or 'limo', in which we would have the client. The third vehicle was called the CAT (counter-assault team vehicle) by some, although we preferred 'gunship', the infantry term for a helicopter. To us, this best described the action this vehicle would take, and it was usually fitted with a PKM machine gun. It gave the team the firepower.

The AKs proved to be rather challenging: specifically, where to place it for ease of operation. It was hardly designed to be handled inside a vehicle. For the shooter, the best position was on the left against the console. This would allow ease of exit in an emergency but it did mean having to shoot left-handed if the threat was on the right. To shoot right-handed meant swivelling right and shifting left to accommodate the rifle's length. This was something we would have to practise on the range. Being able to lay down effective fire on attackers in any contact was critical. And the quicker this happened, the less chance there was of casualties. The last thing you wanted was to lose a client.

And on that checklist of undesirable outcomes, the next was a vehicle accident. To keep security contracts you needed vehicles, you needed reliable vehicles, and you needed a clean record.

Despite the risen sun, it was still freezing cold, and snow covered the mountains all the way along the route. The going wasn't fast, as the road running north between Kirkuk and Mosul was busy with slow-moving Humvees escorting convoys of trucks. The Humvees were US infantry vehicles mounted with a gun turret and a 50-calibre Browning machine gun, and manned by five soldiers. In any convoy the last vehicle had a sign reading: 'Danger stay back 100 m'.

Effectively, this meant we couldn't overtake a Humvee convoy. Not exactly a prime position to be in when you were in a hurry. There was nothing for it but to wait until the convoy turned off. What we did learn was that we would have to factor this into future missions. I'd been told that if you got too close to a Humvee they would throw water bottles at you until you fell back. If you didn't respond they would open fire. A 50-calibre Browning machine gun can make a mess of any car and it was certainly not an event I wished to experience.

We went through out first roadblocks on that mission but these were uneventful as they were Peshmerga-manned. Our Peshmerga drivers did warn us that in Baghdad we would need DoD badges, because without them getting through a checkpoint could be difficult. I was amused at the way they spoke of Iraq as if it were another country. But I held my tongue and didn't point out that this territory was as much a part of Iraq as was Baghdad.

While mostly the trip followed standard military procedures for vehicle movement, we did realise that there was one major difference: in military manoeuvres your objective was to kill the enemy; in client protection you wanted to avoid contact with the enemy. In those days there were not many who had any form of VIP protection training. Casper was one of the few who had been through the SAP Task Force training.

We realised, too, that communication was going to be a top priority in any emergency. To enable this, we would need earpieces for the mobile radios to ensure our hands were free to use weapons or shepherd clients out of danger. Earpieces also meant that radio contact in the limo would be inaudible to the client, which would prevent unnecessary panic. We took Casper's advice here but I also decided to trawl the internet for any training manuals or articles on protection services work. We realised how critical the radios were going to be, and I hoped to heaven that Mauritz had managed to get them through the border.

He had. He and John arrived early in the afternoon, pleased that they'd been able to negotiate the border crossing without incident. Excited and relieved that we had the radios, we loaded up and dished out weapons and body armour. We wanted to take an alternative route for the return journey, but the Peshmerga drivers told us there was only the one road. This was against our training – using the same route in and out of a place was just not done.

John Walbridge, co-owner of OSSI/Safenet.

By the time we got to Mosul it was early evening and the traffic was bad (it would get even worse in the next few years). As we approached a major traffic circle we heard shots but couldn't determine their origin. Immediately we were on the alert, weapons ready, a round in the chamber, safety catch off. Out the corner of my eye I noticed Mauritz bringing his weapon up to fire.

I glanced at the possible target: a policeman running towards us. Clearly, Mauritz had no idea of the man's position.

'Policeman,' I screamed. 'Stop, Mauritz!'

He lowered his weapon and the policeman ran past us into the crowd, unaware of our reaction.

My nerves were on edge until we'd cleared the city and the traffic opened up. Then I could feel the three of us relax.

'That was close,' said Mauritz.

'No kidding.' I blew out a breath. 'Wouldn't have been a good start to your Iraq adventure.'

But it did teach us a lesson: when a new guy came into the country he would need a thorough briefing. No one wanted a blue-on-blue incident (army lingo for own forces against each other.)

The next day John gave us an update on the proposal he had submitted for security work on the telecommunications project. It was in the area and that was why we were based in Sulaymaniyah for the time being.

In the morning we also organised a shopping expedition to the local arms market in town. An extraordinary place, with everything you could wish for laid out in the sun on mats, carpets and boxes. There were assault rifles, handguns, grenades, RPGs, body armour, webbing, ammunition of every calibre. Some of the weapons were knock-offs, but there were also weapons from well-known manufacturers.

I had never seen anything like it. Military weapons fairs in Western countries are one thing, the informality of this marketplace was something else altogether. It was the arms dealer's version of a farmer's market.

We soon had all the equipment we needed, webbing mostly, and the tools Rieme wanted to fit the radios into the vehicles. Rieme was good at anything mechanical or where welding was involved. His skills were invaluable to the team during our start-up phase. To celebrate, our interpreter took us to a place he knew that sold shawarmas. At first I was sceptical, as the ones sold near the hotel were superb, but I went with his suggestion and was not disappointed.

The ever-handy Rieme de Jager (centre) fits the radios in the Nissan Patrols. On the right is Snoeks Niewhoud giving advice.

After lunch, the vehicles that Casper had acquired through the same interpreter's family arrived. They were second-hand but in good condition. By late afternoon, Rieme had them fitted out with the radios.

All we needed now were the weapons that Casper had acquired. These arrived the next morning in the form of MP5s. Not a standard weapon in the South African Army, but it was used by the Special Forces. The beauty of it was that, like most Heckler & Koch weapons, it was simple to operate, clean to maintain, and came with five magazines. As mentioned, where the MP5 had an advantage over the AK-47 was in a vehicle. When the butt was not extended, it was easy to handle in a confined space.

My only misgivings, as I've said, were with the 9 mm calibre. From my experience with these weapons, they didn't pack sufficient punch in a critical situation. When I was in 31 Battalion we'd tested the power of 9 mm bullets and found that they didn't always penetrate a car door. For me this was an issue only partly compensated for by their ease of handling.

To make up for this lack of firepower, we did have the Russian PKM machine gun, and some 800 rounds of ammunition in belts. The calibre was 7.62 x 59R, of Eastern European origin, which in my books was fantastic. All in all, we were well kitted up. The body armour was South African and gave us protection up to 7.62 x 51 calibre.

Former soldiers like nothing more than spending time on the range shooting, and we scheduled this for the following day. Breakfast was wolfed down amid great excitement, and then we piled into the vehicles and headed for the shooting zone, an old building outside the town. There we set up a range facing the mountains, placed boxes as targets with an earth wall behind them and got down to the serious business of zeroing the weapons. It didn't take long. In this Rieme was the lead, as he was a sniper and highly knowledgeable about weapons and weapon training. Snoeks and I took charge of range procedures and safety.

For Eddie, this was his first time out with the MP5. It's a great little weapon, accurate and easy to handle from all positions, with very little recoil. Even on full automatic you can keep the grouping on the target. It didn't take long to get Eddie up to speed.

The moment we were all anticipating was firing the PKM. I've had some experience with these weapons and knew they were prone to stoppages if a cartridge failed or the belt was dirty. You had to keep the belt clean at all times. A cartridge failure meant clearing it from the chamber, and for that you needed a ramrod, not necessarily a quick operation. In a tight spot a replacement barrel was the best option.

Our team of intrepid travellers on the shooting range outside Sulaymaniyah in Iraqi Kurdistan.

For our first shooting the PKM fired perfectly, in fact so accurately that we did not have to adjust the sights. We all took turns firing the weapon, another first for Eddie who by now looked like an old pro. The most important thing he had to learn was that when unloading the weapon it left a round in the feeder, even if the belt was detached. Imagine the disturbance in an armoured vehicle if that shot were fired by mistake. Not something any of us were keen to experience.

At close quarters, the **PKM** will penetrate an armoured vehicle. Load up with armour-piercing rounds and they'll cut through an armoured vehicle like the proverbial hot knife through butter. These rounds were also used by the Russian-made Dragunov sniper rifles, but then the Russians liked manufacturing weapons that fired the same ammunition, as this made supply so much easier. For instance, both the **RPD** and **RPK** machine guns used the AK-47 round, 7.62 x 39.

At the end of a successful and enjoyable day we stopped in at the arms bazaar to buy some tools for vehicle repairs: trolley jacks to enable us to change flat tyres quickly, wheel spanners with a torque wrench so that we wouldn't struggle to loosen or tighten nuts. No one wanted to lose a wheel at high speed. In addition, we stocked up with jumper cables, spare batteries, spare fan and aircon motor belts, engine and transmission oil, brake fluid. Let alone spanners, pliers, screwdrivers, cable ties. And decent toolboxes for each vehicle.

For the next ten days we did some serious training. We practised our first firing from stationary vehicles, followed by live runs with the vehicles moving. We also practised cross-loading clients from one vehicle to another in case the limo was damaged or broke down (at this point we used only two vehicles). But it was one thing going through these motions ourselves; we needed to experience cross-loading with real clients. John and Mauritz proved excellent dummies.

As their weapons had to be tested, and they required shooting practice wearing body armour, we bundled them into the lead vehicle one day and headed for the range. (Wearing body armour was a new thing for us. If back in the Border War we'd had to wear what the American soldiers were wearing in Iraq, we would surely have lost the war. There was no way we could have lasted a day under South West African sun if we'd had to slog around with body armour, a helmet and our kit.)

John immediately wanted to know why we were transporting 'clients' in the lead vehicle. This had been a contentious issue throughout our training, with Casper insisting that the client had to be in the second vehicle. The rest of us argued that we could not support the clients if they were behind us in the second vehicle – an argument John appreciated.

After the ten days the team was fully operational. All we needed were clients. And although there was a shortage of security teams, finding clients was not that easy. John had since heard that he'd not been successful in winning the telecommunications contract.

Everyone we had spoken to told us all the work was in Baghdad – that was where we had to get to. We decided that we would leave for the capital city as soon as possible. Casper would stay behind in Kurdistan in case another opportunity in that part of the country came up.

And that is where we headed, taking the interpreter with us because the maps were useless and we needed someone who knew the road to Baghdad and could also help us find a decent hotel.

4
Reconnoitring Baghdad

We left early in the morning for Baghdad. I was unsure how many checkpoints there would be but I had done some internet research and selected a number of hotels in the centre of the city where we would probably find accommodation. We needed hotels where we could take the weapons into the rooms, where the vehicles would be in a secure parking area – not on the street, as we had heard too many stories of car bombs and IEDs (improvised explosive devices) going off in the streets. As there was no longer any fighting in the city, I worked on the premise that driving around would not be too hazardous. With the interpreter to ease our way, I was not expecting any difficulties.

We had packed the vehicles the night before and each of us carried a weapon, body armour and a small bag of clothes and toiletries. The interpreter arrived half an hour later than our scheduled departure time, which was frustrating but we were soon enough out of town and on the road. Rieme, Snoeks and the interpreter were in the front vehicle; Eddie and I behind. The PKM machine gun was on the back seat of our vehicle.

One of the issues with long-distance travel was the lack of petrol stations. Instead, fuel was sold in 25-litre cans on the side of the road. The only indication of a petrol point was a guy waving a funnel. Interestingly, Iraqi petrol was colourless. If it had so much as a tinge of colour we dismissed it as poor quality.

About halfway to Baghdad we encountered our first checkpoint at what was the Iraqi-Kurdish 'border'.

One of the many informal fuel points along the road to Baghdad.

'You see,' I said to Eddie, in some exasperation. 'They really do think this is another country.'

The border guards asked for our passports but we could see they did not know what they were looking for. The guard who had my passport looked long and hard at my Angolan visa. Most troops, we were to learn, could neither read nor write, and few could understand English. Checkpoints were always interesting places, and 14 years later this was still true. Soon enough we were waved through.

Approaching Baghdad and with our fuel low, we stopped at one of the roadside fuel points outside the city. There the guy selling petrol asked whether we wanted to refuel the main or the sub (reserve) tank. I looked at the fuel inlet and saw the two pipes. I told him to fill up only the main tank, but the moment I got into the car I looked it up in the manual. It had all the information: when the main tank was low, we only had to push a button and the fuel in the sub-tank would flow into the main.

Damn, I felt so stupid. How many more things would we have to learn? Embarrassment aside, at least this meant that we had a significant range in the vehicles, which was a decided advantage.

Once we were on our way again, I asked Rieme on the radio if the interpreter could find out from some of the locals walking along the road how we could locate a hotel in the city. After a few seconds Rieme indicated for us to pull over.

Problem. The interpreter could neither speak Arabic nor did he know Baghdad.

I lost it. 'Get out of the car,' I shouted at him, 'and get your arse back to Casper.'

This was all we needed: a city we didn't know where we didn't speak the language.

'Here.' I thrust $50 at the interpreter so he could pay for a taxi. 'Why the hell didn't you tell us this before we set out.' But it was no good remonstrating with him. He just stared at the ground.

We left him standing there on the side of the road and drove towards the centre of Baghdad on the main highway from Tadji. The only clue we were headed in the right direction was the Tigris River, which bisects the city.

At the bridge over the river was the inevitable checkpoint.

'This is going to be fun,' I muttered to Eddie.

As things turned out, a captain at the roadblock had enough English to direct us to a hotel, the Al Hamra, not far away.

'What's their case?' I said to Eddie. I didn't like having guns pointed at me and it was all I could do to restrain myself from retaliating.

One of the guards shouted at us in Arabic and we shouted back, 'English, English. Get someone who can speak English.' He snapped something into his radio and the next minute there was a Brit striding through the checkpoint towards us.

A typical checkpoint in Baghdad. This one, near the airport, was manned by a local security company.

'Well, hello,' he said. 'Where the hell did you lot come from? And who are you, for that matter?'

We told him.

'Welcome. Welcome. There're plenty of rooms here,' he said, waving at the guards to let us in. Which they did after they'd mirror-searched underneath the vehicles.

'Do you work for the hotel?' I asked while the guards did their job.

'Heavens, no. I'm with CNN television. But we help out with security. In our best interests to do so.'

He showed us where to park the vehicles and shepherded us to reception.

This was fascinating. There was a metal detector at the entrance similar to the ones in airports. We handed our weapons to the guard, walked through the detector, and our weapons were returned to us on the other side.

'Now what the fuck was the point of that?' I asked.

The Brit just laughed.

The Al Hamra was a hotel with a main highrise building and an annex that was only three storeys tall. In between was a swimming pool, apparently the largest in the city. We were shown accommodation in the annex, where the rooms were more like apartments, with a lounge, kitchen and two bedrooms with two beds in each.

This was ideal. Mauritz was going to be with us on and off, as was John, and there would be accommodation for them when they did stop over. The lounge I determined would be the operational centre – a grandiose title as we had not much more than a spare radio with which to equip it. But that would change as we acquired maps, laptops and other equipment.

With a sense of anticipation we unpacked and headed downstairs to a dining room, which was rowdy with CNN reporters and staff, and locals who worked for them. I found out that they occupied the two top floors of the hotel tower block and had been in the country for some time. We pulled up a table in this magnificent dining room, which was Arabic in style, with heavy drapes, carpets, big wooden furniture and ornaments on every surface.

A few tables away I noticed another personal security detail (PSD) team. They looked American but kept to themselves and seemed almost to shy away from the press. I noticed that they carried sidearms under their jackets. At another table sat CNN's British security team. They were more relaxed and didn't stick out as obviously as the American team.

There were other guests in the dining room but they were all civilians.

'I can't see that they'll be much use to us,' said Rieme, indicating the local businessmen.

'Don't knock them, china,' I responded. 'They're exactly the guys we're looking for. One of them could be a contract in the making.'

'Ja,' he conceded. 'You're probably right.'

We ordered dinner, not knowing what we were letting ourselves in for. What we were served was a pleasant surprise. It would've been nice to wash it down with a beer but before we left South Africa we'd decided that the company would have a non-alcoholic policy in Iraq. It being a Muslim country for one thing; for another, guns and alcohol don't mix. Water and coffee would come to be our main liquid refreshments. A lot of water it would turn out, as the moment you sat down in a restaurant water would be brought to the table. The coffee was good too – Nescafé, but we were used to this. At the end of the meal I signed the chit, which was to become standard procedure as the accounts were my responsibility.

Now that we were settled and had eaten I was keen to return to my running regime. It seemed to me the only places available were the staircases of the two hotel buildings. This would be a serious challenge.

The staircases were dusty and looked like they hadn't been cleaned or used in a while. But that was a small drawback.

I changed into my running gear and did a few laps round the pool to warm up before tackling the annex staircase. Three

For the first few months of our time in Baghdad we stayed at the Al Hamra Hotel. It had one of the best pools in the city and was a great place to make new contacts.

storeys were easy, and I was hardly taking strain when I went onto the roof, hoping for a view of the city. But no horizons were visible; I was surrounded by taller buildings.

I now headed for the twelve-storey tower block. This was a different ball game altogether. Although I tried to maintain a steady pace, halfway up I realised that no ways was this going to happen. Fortunately, there was a landing on each floor which gave my legs some respite.

From the sixth floor my legs ached, and all I could think about was getting to the next landing. Despite the cold, I was soon drenched with sweat. Gasping for breath, I staggered through the roof door onto the top of the building. As I heaved and panted, I marvelled at the view. I could see large sections of the city centre, and across the river to where I believed the Green Zone lay. The heavily fortified Green Zone was home to the Coalition Provisional Authority, which ran the country after the 2003 invasion. Access was possible only through a handful of control points.

Once I'd steadied my breathing I headed back down the stairs, which, if anything, was more painful than the ascent. It killed my legs, and I envied the guests sitting around the pool drinking coffee. I made it back to the room I shared with Eddie intent on a shower and then some time relaxing beside the pool.

'Hey, Neil, you okay, man?' asked Eddie as I entered the room, my breath in ragged gasps, my gear soaked with sweat. 'You look like you're gonna have a heart attack.' His face was all consternation.

'It was tough,' I managed to get out. 'You wanna join me anytime, you're welcome.'

'You gotta be kidding,' he said, going back to his magazine.

I told him about the gathering place around the pool, and after I'd showered we went down and ordered coffee.

'You don't know who you can meet down here,' I said. 'It's the place to bump into people.'

There was a group of journos, young, loud and totally relaxed, and then other diplomatic types in their suits and ties. Aside from them were some businessmen and executives, smartly dressed, but a lot less formally, and certainly not at ease. People had their laptops out or, in the case of the diplomatic guys, were talking earnestly with their local contacts.

Eddie and I drank coffee and observed the scene.

We hadn't been there long when the other PSD team approached us. They were friendly enough and wanted to know where we were from and what company we worked for. I told them.

'Look,' said one of them, 'we're off to the Green Zone now, where they've got a gym. We're with a company called Blackwater that handles most of the security work for the US embassy. Let's get together. We'll show you the ropes.'

'Appreciate that,' I said.

Blackwater rang a bell. I'd heard about the company, but back then it was nowhere near the world's most powerful private army it was to become.

'If we get half a chance we need to pick their brains,' I said to Eddie. 'Could give us a useful head start.'

As the cold of evening was drawing in we decided to call it quits. It'd been a long and eventful day and there was a tension in Baghdad that was palpable, it ran like a current through everyone. If a waiter dropped a cup, the tension quickly surfaced, everybody seemed poised to dive for cover. The threat was everywhere around us, up close and in your face.

The next morning at breakfast we bumped into the Blackwater guys again and introduced them to the rest of our team. When they said they would be going to the Green Zone shortly, I asked them what we had to do to get access to the zone.

'Do you have a DoD [US Department of Defense] badge or anything like that?' one of them asked.

'No, we only have our passports,' I said.

'I'm afraid you'll need either an embassy or DoD badge to get in.'

'So, where do we get one of those?'

He then explained that we would need to get a direct contract with the American government or be a prime contractor of the government. However, there was also the option of a weekly visit permit if you could get a sponsor to confirm that you had legitimate business in the Green Zone. Our new friend at Blackwater then offered to find out on our behalf how this permit worked.

Our first tasks that day were to recce the hotel's surrounds and the access streets and to locate a shop that sold cold drinks, chips and cigarettes. Life has its priorities and fortunately there was a handy minimarket close by. We also realised that the whole neighbourhood, including three other hotels, seemed to be part of the hotel's security compound.

Also, we were lucky to score maps from the Blackwater team who were moving into accommodation in the Green Zone. These included the latest aerial photomaps of the whole of Baghdad, and finely detailed street maps that would allow us to plan our routes. Our control room began to look like a serious centre of operations.

Another consideration was to have an easily accessible exit should the hotel come under fire. We decided to park the vehicles directly below our rooms and use a rope to abseil from the room's balcony in an emergency. Then we each needed a 'grab bag' of essential provisions that could be snatched up in a crisis: things such as bandages, pain pills, ammunition, compass, cable ties, water and tinned food.

Over time the contents of the bag changed as we gained more experience and also started using other equipment such as GPS units and satellite phones. On our first trip back to South Africa we bought GPSes and these had a huge impact on our route planning and navigation. Most importantly, it meant we didn't have to rely solely on an Iraqi driver to get from point A to point B.

Another urgent consideration was a translator. I asked the hotel clerk if he knew of anyone and it turned out his cousin was a possibility. The man was in his mid-twenties, had completed a year's military service and had studied botany and English at university. He could also speak Kurdish. His name was Hassan Salam and we hired him for $350 a month until we landed a contract and could afford to pay more.

Prior to a day spent reconnoitring the city with Hassan, we spent time studying the maps and air photos given to us by the Blackwater guys. We divided the city into three regions – northern, central and southern – and then worked out how to get onto the main highways to major cities in Iraq. Interestingly, the route to the airport – as most other major routes – was called something different by the US military: ASR or Route Irish. I eventually learnt ASR stood for 'alternative supply route'. The highways were designated MSR, or 'main supply routes'. We needed to memorise these as well as the

It was rarely easy getting around in the congested Baghdad traffic.

A street scene in Bagdad, with women (left) in burkas and men in traditional clothing.

official names if we were going to work with the Americans. And if the gift of the maps was anything to go by, we were in with a fighting chance.

The next morning we set out with Hassan for the Green Zone but via the airport. He cautioned that Route Irish was dangerous, as IEDs were placed in dead animals and cellphones were used to explode the devices when a PSD team passed. Their accuracy wasn't great but I was sure this would change over time and they would become more deadly. Rieme and Snoeks took the lead vehicle with Hassan, and Eddie and I followed, with Eddie driving. Rieme kept up a steady commentary as we proceeded.

Whenever we encountered other PSD teams we realised that they adopted the American tactics of throwing water bottles if we got too close or would use laser pointers to warn off those who strayed into their safety zone. All of them had notices on the rear warning other road users to stay back. Hassan had already told us some horror stories about trigger-happy guys who thought it was fun taking out errant vehicles. They would shoot and carry on with their mission even if there were wounded people in the target vehicle.

In one instance, where we wanted to overtake a PSD team travelling particularly slowly, the guy in the gunship waved his hands frantically and looked like he was about to shoot. We dropped back. We hadn't brought the PKM machine gun and were certainly not spoiling for a fight. Ours was just a mission to recce the routes.

I noticed that most of the other PSD teams operated three vehicle convoys. Their tactics were slightly different to those we had seen in Kurdistan. Here they would leapfrog each other to block vehicles trying to force their way in from the sides. The client vehicle remained in the middle with the lead and gunship doing the rotating.

Out on Route Irish we ran into a roadblock mounted by the American army. Cars were stationary all over the centre of the highway.

'When the Americans do that it's because of an IED,' said Hassan.

While he was talking, the PSD team in front of us stuck on their hazards and, with sirens blaring, crossed the median into the oncoming traffic.

'Follow,' I radioed to Rieme. 'If that's how they do it, we'll do it too.'

'Be careful,' warned Hassan. 'They shoot if they feel threatened. Sometimes they shoot for no reason.'

I could believe it. These guys were cowboys and they acted as if they ruled the road. They certainly knew how to piss off the locals. I couldn't understand their mentality.

Welcome to Baghdad.

As we approached the airport Hassan advised us to turn around as we didn't have the necessary clearance to enter the airport surrounds. There was a US military checkpoint ahead so we took the slip road and again joined Route Irish, this time in the direction of town.

The rest of the morning we spent becoming *au fait* with other highways and then headed for the Green Zone. Hassan directed us to a turn-off just before the bridge over the river. This took us through a residential area favoured by Iraqi generals to the main checkpoint from the Green Zone onto Route Irish. Here the traffic was dense and we took a while to reach the checkpoint. But, before we did, Hassan had us do a U-turn down a side road as we skirted along the perimeter of the Green Zone.

RECONNOITRING BAGHDAD

This photo shows a T-wall on the right and Hesco barriers in the background. Here we are entering a checkpoint at a forward operating base manned by US forces.

A T-wall – a barrier made of steel-reinforced concrete slabs almost four metres tall – separated the Green Zone from the rest of the city and ran all along the river. The name 'T-wall' was commonly used by US soldiers in Iraq as its cross-sectional shape resembled an inverted letter T.

Looking back from the bridge, we could see into the Green Zone. Other than scaling the T-wall or going through a checkpoint there was no other way into the Green Zone. And going over the T-wall was not an option as there were cameras spaced along its length.

On the way back to the hotel we passed the 14th July Bridge checkpoint, which took its name from the day the Americans launched their attack on the city. This was close to our hotel and meant we were only a few minutes from the Green Zone.

Our plans to reconnoitre the northern sector of Baghdad the next day suddenly changed when Mauritz emailed to say he would be coming in through the Jordanian border. We were to meet him there. Not too much of a problem as there was a six-lane highway linking the border with Baghdad. The only danger points would be the many bridges crossing the highway between Fallujah and Ramadi, according to Hassan.

Out there we would be in the desert where Saddam's supporters had rallied. They were Sunni Muslims and violently opposed to the invasion. A PSD team or an American convoy, they would display the same aggression towards both: everyone was fair game to them.

'They like to shoot down from the bridges,' Hassan informed us. 'Then they chase you to kill and destroy.'

Another issue was fuel. The distance to the border was 600 km and while Hassan was certain there were fuelling points at Ramadi, from there it would be 'dry' until we reached the border – always assuming there actually was fuel at the border. An alternative was to carry drums of fuel in the vehicles, not something any of us fancied as we might be involved in a contact. The only option was to take our chances and refuel at the first opportunity after Fallujah. That would at least give us enough fuel to make it to the border and back. Given a good tar road we could probably travel at 120 km/h and this would certainly test our range on the fuel tanks.

This mission to pick up Mauritz was also important because we believed it would become our main route in and out of Iraq. He would fly into Amman in Jordan, overnight there, and then drive the 300 km to the border with Iraq. If he left at 08:00 and we left at 04:30 we should get to the border at about the same time. For us this meant departing in the dark, which was not a problem: we knew the road and there would be less traffic. By first light we would be close to Fallujah and refuelling points.

The evening before, we topped up the vehicles' tanks at a fuel station not far from the hotel. The moment we arrived, the petrol jockeys recognised us as a PSD team and waved us to the front of the queue.

'What's this about?' I asked Hassan.

'They don't want us to be here for too long,' he replied with a smile. 'For them it is dangerous.'

We took up defensive positions around the vehicles while Hassan ensured that they were properly filled, and the sub-tanks likewise. In future we would get him to handle the refuelling by himself as we weren't at ease standing around with our guns. The lucky – and the lucky included the CNN security team – had passes into the Green Zone where they could fill up without any worries.

While it would have made life easier if we had access to the filling stations in the Green Zone, we had decided that we wanted to follow a low-profile strategy. This meant that we tried to blend in with the local population as much as possible – when we were out on a mission, we wore the same clothes as they did (never a uniform), we drove second-hand cars and even refuelled where they did. Our main aim was to avoid drawing unnecessary attention to ourselves.

We had not been in the country for long, but we had already learnt much simply by watching how other PSD teams operated. In fact, after watching various PSD teams at work escorting clients to and from the hotel we'd decided that low profile had many advantages: your clients were more at ease because they didn't have guys with guns standing over them; and because we didn't stand out nobody could identify us as a security team. This meant we could more effectively protect our clients.

5
The Sunni triangle of death

We left on schedule in the morning. We had snacks for the road and plenty of water, in addition to body armour for Mauritz and an extra gun. Eddie, Snoeks and Hassan were in the lead vehicle; I drove the gunship with Rieme behind the PKM machine gun. We were driving into what was known as the Sunni triangle of death and could not afford to take chances.

We were testing the hand-held radios with earpieces, and this worked well as Rieme was able to keep us informed of any threat from the rear. We made good time in the dark, and, if we had any advantage at all, it was that any 'bad guys' would not be able to identify us as a PSD team until it was too late. As most PSD teams moved in three- or four-vehicle convoys, a two-up looked more like taxis travelling together, even though we were in the Nissan Patrols, which drew unnecessary attention.

We passed Fallujah at first light and entered the notorious triangle of death, stopping at a small shop on the outskirts of Ramadi to refuel and to buy breakfast: cold drinks, chips and biscuits.

As business was slack at the fuelling stop at that time of the morning, we were quickly done and on our way. The next town was Ramadi and then it was empty desert. We upped the speed to average 140 km/h.

On the road through the desert the only vehicles were trucks and taxis. The trucks coming from Jordan were laden with second-hand vehicles and vegetables. There weren't many

THE SUNNI TRIANGLE OF DEATH

military convoys, as they preferred to move at night. This made sense because they would be less vulnerable in the dark and the quality of their night-vision equipment was excellent.

In all that desert sand the strangest sights were flocks of sheep being led by a shepherd, the way it was recorded in the Bible.

'Why do the shepherds lead the sheep?' I asked Hassan over the radio.

'Because the sheep are short and cannot see where there is grass,' he replied. 'They need the shepherd to take them to their food.' This made sense, but even all these years later I am still intrigued by the sight.

If the sheep provided an amusing interlude, then the aftermath of IED attacks were a reminder of where we were travelling. These attacks left holes on the side of the road and caused damage to the road surface too. Then there were the burnt and shot-up vehicles, evidence of ambushes. In these empty vastnesses it was hard to believe these moments of terror and possibly death had occurred.

We arrived at the border earlier than anticipated, which gave us time to refuel and relax at a restaurant selling chicken kebabs and chai. An hour later we met Mauritz in the parking lot as agreed.

Much against my better judgement he asked to drive until Ramadi to get a feel for the vehicle.

'Ja, okay.' I said. 'But we need to go a bit faster now to get back before dark.' The last thing I wanted was being stuck behind a military convoy at night.

Going fast translated to Mauritz as 170 km/h. At that speed there was no way our fuel would last to Baghdad. I got on the radio and told him to slacken off to 150 km/h and we settled on that as our cruising speed until the denser traffic volumes near Baghdad slowed us down.

With some relief, about thirty minutes later we pulled into the parking area at the Al Hamra Hotel.

Mauritz always brought goodies from South Africa. On this occasion he brought *mieliepap* (mielie meal). We immediately decided that the next day's mission would be to find a butchery. These *boere* were going to braai.

Hassan directed us to a butcher near the Al Warda market. As our rooms were self-catering we'd been buying our groceries there to save money because eating in the hotel dining room each day was expensive. Al Warda stocked plenty of Western brands, and, most importantly, Nescafé coffee. However, the stock of spices was limited.

Long-life milk was the only milk available. Iraqis drank *leben*, a sour milk from the water buffalo that was sold on the side of the road. This was the only fresh dairy product available. As far as other provisions were concerned, their vegetables and fruit were imported from Turkey and Jordan and this was of good quality and plentiful. Today you can buy South African fruit, mostly bananas and oranges, in the bigger markets, but things were more basic back in 2003.

As Hassan knew the butcher, we were all geared up to buy some excellent cuts.

But.

We were soon to find out that a butchery in Baghdad differed in many respects from butcheries in South Africa. Animals were slaughtered in the street outside the shop, and as a result the air was thick with flies. Nor did the butcher neatly cut the meat into steaks, chops, etc. No, he hacked it into pieces with a machete.

We considered this a cardinal sin. We did not want our meat hacked to pieces like this. Imagine cooking those chunks on a braai?

We rarely missed an opportunity to have a braai. This was our first braai on the Camp Rustamiyah project, a few months after our arrival in Iraq.

By the time we got there that morning the butcher had already sold out of meat. We explained that we wanted half a sheep and asked if he had a saw. He had no such implement and couldn't understand why we wanted one. We decided to take our chances on his butchering skills.

The next morning we arrived to find he had not done a good job of preparing our cuts. Rieme tried to explain how we wanted the meat, but the guy had been cutting meat this way all his life as had his father and his father's father before him. No one was about to change to suit the tastes of a bunch of

South Africans. We decided that in future we would get to his butchery early and cut up the sheep ourselves; we felt passionately that it should be done the right way.

Back at the hotel, it was time for Operation Meat. All we had available to cut up the meat chunks into recognisable steaks was a hacksaw. It did the job and it wasn't long before the braai meat was spiced and marinated and the rest packed and in the freezer.

I should add that in later years we acquired a bandsaw, which I still use today. It made our meat purchases easier, as we could buy a back leg or half a cow and butcher and package it ourselves. This way we were sure of getting the best T-bone steaks. Apart from the fat-tailed sheep the butcheries sold, it was possible to buy beef but this was not as freely available and you had to get to the markets very early in the morning if you wanted to secure a cut. A common meat was buffalo but it was not a taste I fancied. However, when there was nothing else we'd buy buffalo. Camel was also available but scarce and expensive.

Now it was braai time. While the meat marinated we set about building a braai on the balcony. Hassan had acquired some charcoal from the local market. It didn't look of good quality but we had seen it being used to grill chickens on the street. For firelighters we used tea bags soaked in petrol. Fortunately this didn't create too much smoke, as we didn't want anyone worried that we'd set the room alight.

The charcoal was on a tray between two chairs. The grill was suspended between these chairs over the coals. The only problem was when we piled on the meat, the chairs tipped and the meat almost landed in the fire. Because Rieme and Snoeks were the braai masters, the only way to sort out this problem was for Eddie and me to sit on the chairs to prevent them from falling over.

Rieme stood back, satisfied. 'Just a pity we don't have a few whiskies and beers to make us feel really at home,' he lamented.

True enough, but you can't have everything. What we did have was a really nice braai complete with the mieliepap Mauritz supplied. Mieliepap, I've always thought, finishes off a braai.

A typical street food stall in Baghdad where we could buy chicken for lunch and supper. You had to get there early or else the chicken would be overcooked.

And it was a welcome change from the tinned food and chicken we'd been living off for the past few days. In Iraq you could get a roasted chicken plus bread and salad for three dollars. It was the cheapest meal you could buy, and it fed four guys at least. Most of the chicken was brought in from Iran and Turkey. Whenever I'm back at home, my family knows that chicken is a no-no. I had and have my fill of it at work.

That Friday braai started a tradition, and even today the few remaining South Africans will gather on a Friday for a braai.

6
Setting up the company

With Mauritz in Baghdad, the two of us discussed opening a bank account for the company. This would allow him and John to transfer money to us in case of an emergency. One of the local banks had a branch in the hotel and I decided to try my luck, with Hassan in tow to interpret. The female bank manager was very helpful and actually spoke some English.

She explained that to open a business account we needed a business licence from the Ministry of Trade (MOT). However, to open a personal account she only needed a copy of my passport and visa. Without much hassle I then opened a dollar and a dinar account. Now at least we had an account if we needed to transfer money. I could also collect a chequebook later that day.

I told Hassan our next priority would be to get the MOT licence and asked him to go to the MOT as soon as possible to find out which forms had to be completed.

Hassan came back with the news that to register the company as a branch office of OSSI and Safenet required a mountain of paperwork. This included a set of registration documents from the country in which the mother company was registered. These documents had to be stamped by the Department of Home Affairs in South Africa and an Iraqi embassy (the closest one was in Jordan).

We also needed financial statements for the two companies for the last five years, which had to be signed off by a registered chartered accountant in the country of registration. On top of this, we would have to appoint an accountant in Iraq and a lawyer. Having these two professionals on board would set us back $1 400 a month. Initially, these would be names on the company documents that would be renewed with the licence renewal each year.

Hassan Salam (centre) became our irreplaceable translator, guide and fixer in Baghdad. Iraqi co-workers Omar (left) and Arkan (background) are also shown.

Later on it would also become obligatory for all foreign companies to pay social security for their local employees. It came down to 17% of an Iraqi guard's salary. The company was issued with a blue book by the MOT in which we had to enter social security deposits and they ratified the entries. Once we started employing locals, I placed this administration in Hassan's hands.

Another issue that I raised with Mauritz was insurance. There was a strong possibility that one of us might be killed in this volatile country, and we needed to be covered. We also needed insurance to pay for the repatriation of bodies or for the reissue of passports should one be lost. Mauritz had worked with Executive Outcomes in various countries, so he was well aware of the insurance implications.

The next priority was somewhere staff could get treated for illnesses or wounds. Hassan suggested the nearby Christian Nuns Hospital, and Eddie and I did a quick inspection. We found it clean and organised and well protected. The doctor we spoke to was fluent in English and gave us a quick tour of the facility. I was impressed.

Back in the vehicle, Eddie and I exchanged notes. He was pleased and thought it better than a lot of government hospitals in South Africa.

We also checked out the Sheikh Zayed Hospital, which was a disaster. Chaos. Patients in the passageways, a trauma room that looked like a butchery. No way was it suitable.

To this day I still use the Christian Nuns.

Our next mission was to fetch John at the Jordanian border. This was planned more or less as it had been when we collected Mauritz except that we left later. Mauritz was not one for getting up and away in the dark.

At the first petrol stop we learnt that there was no petrol at the border, which was a problem. It meant we'd have to do over a thousand kilometres before we could refuel. I wasn't sure the vehicles had that sort of range.

There was nothing for it but to carry on and hope that there was fuel somewhere along the route. We reduced our cruising speed to 120 km/h, as this gave us the best fuel economy. If we had a quarter tank in hand plus the spare tank by the time we got to the border we had a fighting chance of making it back without having to refuel. Halfway to the border we spotted a fuel point that was open and pulled in to top up the tanks. I reckoned that we'd probably be able to refuel here on the way back, as no one had yet realised this fuel station had petrol.

In those days Iraq did not have a cellphone network. Had there been cellphones, the word would have got out about this refuelling point and their storage tanks would have been sucked dry in no time. Cellphones would have a major effect on the war in Iraq. Communications were instant and, more seriously, cellphones could be used to detonate roadside bombs. Radios were being used as triggers in 2003, but they were less effective and the bombers had to be a lot closer to the device.

Once we'd refuelled we upped our speed in order to make up for lost time. As it was we were 45 minutes late. John arrived at the border minutes before us and we introduced him to Hassan.

The other taxi drivers asked Hassan whether there was fuel along the route. Word soon got out that we had indeed refuelled, and the taxis that had been stuck at the border for days took off. We had no hope of travelling at their speeds (never under 160 km/h) and, besides, there were drift sands on the road – the last thing you wanted was to hit those patches at speed. I had seen the result of trucks that had driven into drift sands at speed and had flipped and rolled. Not something we wanted to experience.

Fortunately we were able to refuel at the same stop again and could now comfortably make it back to Baghdad. Except that we had to be on high alert after Ramadi, as there'd been more burnt-out trucks and IED holes along the road than we'd encountered when fetching Mauritz. We could only really stand down when we reached the hotel. Without a doubt we would all have been happier in an armoured vehicle because we were exposed and vulnerable in a so-called soft skin.

Back at the hotel, I briefed John about what was required to open a business bank account and that we would have to register our company. We also wanted to join an organisation called the Private Security Company Association of Iraq, which met in the Green Zone weekly to discuss matters affecting the industry. The catch-22 was that you had to have a DoD badge to get into the Green Zone.

'Let me sort it,' said John. 'I've got a colleague in the embassy and I said I'd make contact.'

This was good news and we set off for dinner in high spirits. With John's guidance, the mysteries of the hotel menu were also revealed. As he was more widely travelled than us, he knew most of the dishes and could tell us what they were. I took a great liking to brinjals, especially in an Iraqi salad. That and freshly baked bread were winners.

Bread in Iraq was great when it was fresh. For breakfast Hassan would bring in freshly baked samoons – a flat diamond-shaped bread found mostly in Iraq – which we smothered in honey and cheese. With coffee it was delicious. We soon found that bread baked in wood-fired ovens tasted the best but, as with all Iraqi bread, you had to eat it fresh as it soon dried out and became hard.

We tried freezing it, which halfway solved the problem. Thawing it out gradually was impossible as it simply became rock-hard. The only alternative was to microwave it in a plastic bag. Such were the travails of the security guys in foreign lands!

The next morning, John brought us up to speed on the company's business prospects. He had five clients interested in looking for business opportunities in Iraq. And he was meeting with his embassy contact that afternoon.

The possibility of five clients presented a number of challenges: we didn't have enough vehicles; we would have to accommodate clients in adjacent rooms on the same floor of the Al Hamra; we would have to station a night guard; we needed more body armour.

The vehicles were the major problem. Hiring taxis offered one solution. Taxi drivers would know the town, and we would not be liable for any damage to their vehicles as we'd be hiring them at their daily rate. Of course, their vehicles were marked by a red number plate, but we could always reassure our clients that the number plate was a ploy to fool the insurgents. The bad guys tended not to target local taxis. If the clients needed to go out at night, we would use our own vehicles.

Mauritz in the ops room would control our missions with these clients, and we would need someone on the roof of the main building to ensure that we had radio coverage.

'I think we should move to the main hotel block,' Rieme said as we discussed these options. 'As high up as possible. That way, we've got some radio coverage when we're driving around town. We also need a radio repeater.'

He was right. A radio repeater is a combination of a receiver and a transmitter that can receive a weak signal and retransmit it at a higher power. With a radio repeater we would have coverage for almost the whole of Baghdad. It now headed the shopping list.

That afternoon we moved into two suites on the tenth floor

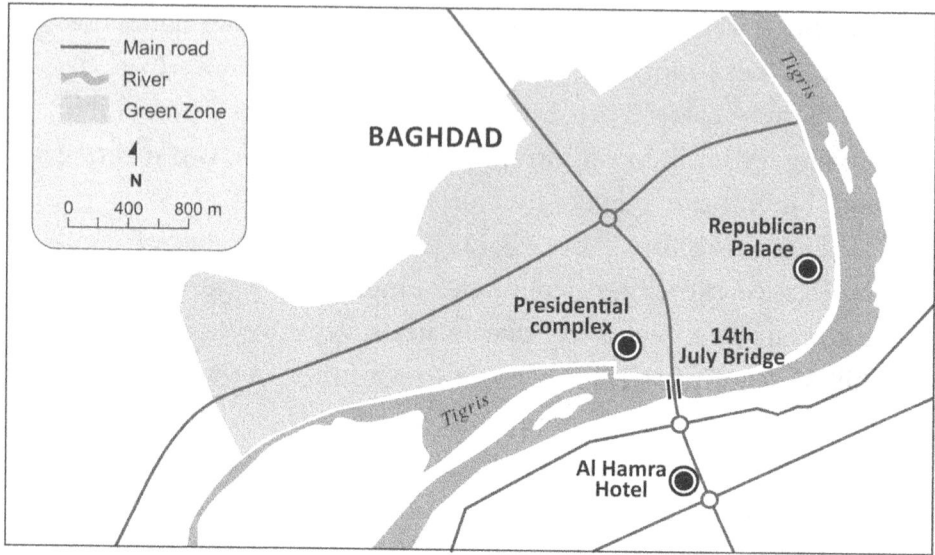

A map of Baghdad showing the Green Zone. The Tigris River divided the Green and Red zones.

of the main building. These were smaller than we'd been used to, but the kitchen was large, modern and well equipped, and there was a view. Another advantage was the consistency of the internet.

No sooner had we installed ourselves in the new suites than it was time to take John to his meeting in the Green Zone. When we arrived at the 14th July checkpoint, John made the US soldiers who manned the checkpoint very jumpy and uptight when he got out of the car. I suspect they thought we carried a car bomb. Fortunately, John's escort was waiting and could defuse the situation.

These young GIs with their guns made me decidedly nervous. They seemed to think everybody was out to kill them, but then they had probably been briefed and trained that way. It was always better to be safe than sorry.

Fetching John was easier, but we were unable to return to

SETTING UP THE COMPANY

the hotel using the counterflow method. This entailed driving, with hazard lights flashing and lights on, the wrong way down the street. Counterflow was accepted practice with the PSD teams, who went by the logic that the least amount of time on the road and the shortest route between two points was absolutely desirable. It was not an option for high-profile teams to be stationary since it made them more vulnerable. We had yet to master the art of being an 'arsehole on the streets', as we were not keen on sticking guns in people's faces unless it was necessary.

From our perspective, John's discussions with his colleague were not entirely successful. He'd learnt that there was business but that the US Department of Defense and Department of State dished out these security contracts. He'd been given a pass to enter the Green Zone at will but was unable to get passes for the rest of us. This did not go down well but we bit our tongues. Obviously, access to the Green Zone would make our lives much easier: apart from the job opportunities, we would be able to get petrol without the worry of being attacked and we could shop for groceries in the American store. We had expected John to come through on this one.

What was also becoming clear now was the tension between John and Mauritz. Partly this was based on financial issues, and I was caught in the crossfire as I controlled and accounted for our expenses. Neither of them could see me as an independent employee. I had never thought that being in control of the finances would be easy, now I foresaw problems ahead. I anticipated other problems, too, such as how to keep the team from choosing sides in any future confrontations between the two owners.

John was with us for only a few days on that trip. Once we'd gone over the company registration necessities again, he spent the rest of the time working the lounge. I had to marvel at the way he could walk up to a table of strangers, introduce himself, and soon get talking to them as if they were long-lost friends.

'You see that,' I said to Eddie as we watched him go through his routine, 'I'm going to have to learn how to do that. Americans are just so much more out there than we are.'

Eddie didn't comment. What could he say, he was one of those hail-fellow-well-met types.

'You know, when I grew up,' I added, 'I was taught not to pester people. Little boys could be seen, not heard. Even as a young man I had to let older people have their say. Just a different way of life, hey!'

7
The contracting business

A couple of nights later we were sitting beside the pool drinking coffee when one of the Blackwater guys approached.

'Some temporary badges for the embassy,' he said holding out the documents. 'All you got to do is fill in your names and they're good for a week. If you come in tomorrow we can meet at the DFAC and I'll show you around.' DFAC was army-speak for the US military's dining facilities.

This was an amazing stroke of luck. These were badges we could renew. We were in. We didn't know how to thank the guy enough.

'You see me in trouble on the road, you better stop,' he joked, waving off our thanks.

First thing the next morning we were on our way to the Green Zone, the land of milk and honey. This day turned out to be a big eye-opener for us.

We had lived outside the wire in the Red Zone since we'd arrived three months previously. We hadn't seen it as a problem and had been careful and ensured that our security was up to standard. Mostly, though, life in the Red Zone hadn't seemed particularly dangerous.

This was not how the personnel who worked in the Green Zone saw the outside. To them the Red Zone was dangerous and everybody was out to kill you. We were somewhat baffled by this but presumed that their briefings and the stories the military and PSD guys brought back fuelled this perception. We knew that most of the PSD talk was just that, talk – stories embellished in the telling. I considered this spin doctoring to make the clients feel there was a need for security, although anybody with a little common sense and experience would know that the stories were often pure fiction. Then again, the way some of the PSD teams drove around I wasn't surprised that the locals took pot shots at them. Blackwater topped the list for this sort of activity.

We arrived at the checkpoint into the Green Zone: Eddie and me in the first vehicle, Rieme and Snoeks following.

The young marine at the checkpoint asked politely for our passports, checked the temporary permits while his companion mirror-searched underneath the vehicle. Next we had to clear the barrels of our weapons before driving the vehicles to a place where they would be searched by sniffer dogs. Doors open, engine hood up, the dogs did their thing. Once they were finished the marine waved us on.

'Easy, hey,' I said to Rieme over the radio. But as if to remind us that this was an oasis in a war zone there was an Abrams tank parked on a bridge overlooking the checkpoint.

At another checkpoint outside the embassy building we were again asked for our badges. This is too easy, I thought, something has to go wrong.

But no. 'Welcome to the embassy,' said the marine.

We were in.

We pulled into the embassy parking area where a number of PSD vehicles were parked, with PSD guys hanging around. At the time, the American embassy was housed in the grand Republican Palace where Saddam Hussein used to meet visiting heads of state.

Ever nonchalant, we hid our weapons under the seats, took off the body armour and headed for the embassy. Without a clue

The 14th July Bridge, which overlooks the checkpoint to the Green Zone. The Abrams tank is visible in the background.

as to the rules and regulations, we decided it best to play safe.

Another checkpoint. We showed our passes.

'Clear the gun barrels of your weapons,' said the marine.

'We're not carrying,' I reassured him.

We were waved through. What immediately caught my eye were the young, good-looking women in civvies, and those in uniform working at the badging office. Then I noticed the interior of the building: marble floors, huge doors, some with gold inlays. The foyer was spacious and doubled as a dining room. There was a serving area with amazing food, including ice cream. You could help yourself to cans of cold drinks – two per person – and snacks and chips. We were too late for breakfast but lunch was served from noon. We were not going to miss out on that!

We sat down at a table, and a few minutes later a group of South African ex-Special Forces guys we knew walked in and joined us. They passed on some useful information, which also helped us to get a better feel for things.

Then came lunch. It was unbelievable. A variety of meats, salads, pastas, burgers and everything in between. On Thursdays we learnt they served fish, lobster and prawns. Never had the South African Army served food like this. They would have been bankrupted just feeding their soldiers at this level.

The Blackwater guys joined us for lunch and suggested we attend the next intelligence briefing, held every morning. It was held in the Regional Security Officer's (RSO) office just down the corridor. All the other security companies attended these briefings. That was where we could renew our badges, and keep up to date with any new embassy regulations.

The Regional Security Officer was usually a high-ranking officer who was in charge of all security regulations at the US embassy and the checkpoints. He had direct influence over the conduct of security companies in the Green Zone, and therefore we needed to be in his good books.

After lunch we wandered round the area and chanced upon the PX (Post Exchange, a type of store found on US military installations across the world.) What we saw inside boggled the mind – it had everything you could wish for. There was a food section, a sweets section and an electronics section where they sold computers and military equipment, although the latter was mostly limited to Leatherman knives, holsters and clothing.

In the food section what caught my eye were the great ribeye steaks and bacon. Bacon, we soon discovered, was a hot item and rapidly sold out. As we had been dying for toast, and Mauritz had brought us a bottle of Marmite, we bought an American loaf in anticipation of a much-missed snack.

THE CONTRACTING BUSINESS

A mural in the Republican Palace depicting Saddam Hussein.

The Republican Palace in the Green Zone served as the US embassy for many years.

The means of exchange was US dollars but they also took credit cards, which was going to make life a lot easier for us.

On the rest of our drive-round we located the main hospital in the Green Zone, a market that sold carpets, paintings and DVDs, some restaurants, and houses that seemed to be occupied by private companies. All were guarded by private security companies.

'How about that?' I said to Eddie. 'Even inside the Green Zone they've got armed guards.'

I realised then that we would have to change our mindset. We were now in the commercial security business and had to sell our services not based on the tactical situation but on the client's budget and the amount of security you could convince them that they needed.

This had been one of our most eventful days in Iraq. It was clear that this 'in' to the Green Zone was going to be significant for our business prospects. Between the embassy and the hotel we had two places where we could meet prospective clients, and I fully expected that the morning intelligence briefing by the Regional Security Officer would also put us into good standing.

A few months after the United States and the Coalition Forces invaded Iraq they began a programme for the reconstruction of the country. International projects were implemented to repair and upgrade Iraqi water and sewage treatment plants, electricity production, hospitals, schools, housing and transportation systems. Much of the work was funded by the US-operated Iraq Relief and Reconstruction Fund, and by the Coalition Provisional Authority.

THE CONTRACTING BUSINESS

US government contracts for construction projects worldwide were listed on a website called Federal Business Opportunities. All you had to do was enter the word Iraq and it would bring up all the projects available in the country. Each construction project needed its own security plan. You could refine the search to security-related opportunities and apply for these. The tender documents were all available electronically as well.

Most of the initial 'discussion' around a project was handled online, but more sensitive information was divulged during site visits and briefings. The sharp PSD team leader would do background research into water availability, electricity connections and the reliability of the power supply during the day and night. They might also send out an Iraqi team member to find out who the local tribal leader was and even to gauge the local communities' responses to the project.

The interested PSD team would take matters further and establish the condition of the roads, the volumes of traffic and how many routes there were to and from the site. In fact, we had a checklist of security questions. All this information would then be passed on to the construction engineers to assist them with their pricing for the bid.

The PSD team's site security proposal would be submitted along with the construction proposal to the military contracting officer. The contract would be awarded taking both these proposals into consideration. Normally, the lowest bid with the best technical proposal would win.

In many instances, construction companies would hire professional proposal-writing companies to compile their proposals, and we went this route too on some of the government contracts. The compiling companies knew the process and the criteria and exactly what the military contracting officers wanted. This could cost anything up to $20 000 but it gave you the best chance of securing the opportunity.

Of course, there were networks within these companies, as many of the compilers were retired military officers who had been involved in the contracting departments and still had contacts and friends within the military. In these instances, the price often went up as your chances of success were greater. As the saying goes, you get what you pay for.

Once a client had secured a contract they would then ask for a detailed security plan, which would include all the standard operating procedures. On bigger projects these also had to be approved by the US military. They would need to know the security measures and the sort of enforcement levels that might be employed. Obviously the security company would be involved in the layout of the site, with the gates being a critical area. Likewise there would need to be watchtowers, lighting and checkpoints. All these had to be indicated on the security drawings. By the time we were finished, a site security plan could easily be a couple of hundred pages long.

Initially, this was a huge amount of work, but as our database expanded it became easier to cut and paste plans from one project to the next. In fact, over time, and as contractors moved from security company to security company, these plans became almost standardised.

There were times when the security situation worsened and we would then have to outline the change in the threat levels and request the use of more personnel and tighter security measures. This motivation would be placed before the military contracting officer. Often the project manager would guide the security provider on the implications for the construction company of heightened threat and security. It was important to have a good relationship with the clients and for them to trust us. Often clients discussed business in the vehicles, and this information was invaluable to PSD team leaders as it gave them a greater understanding of the client's approach.

Our site manager was a critical appointment in this regard. He would have to maintain a good relationship with the client during the project, but, equally importantly, the trust that was built up could influence our being awarded future contracts. This was what we wanted – to be in a position where a construction company defaulted their security work to us.

Sometimes this meant appointing site managers who were great public relations men but not necessarily the best at security. Personality was the key factor here.

There were various ways in which a security company could be involved in a contract. It could be a direct contract with the US government in which you were the prime contractor and were paid directly by the government. This was the best option, as you received all the support you needed from the contracting officer.

With some of the contracts the US government supplied all the security equipment. This included, but was not limited to, weapons, radios and vehicles. Depending on the contract, you could also be provided with meals, flights and medical facilities.

Another way was to operate as a subcontractor to the prime contractor. This meant relying on the client, and sometimes this could be a nightmare if the client was inefficient. This was also the point at which government support stopped. If you ended up being a security provider for a subcontractor there would be no benefits from the government.

If you had only one government contract your company

was made. You could get DoD badges and authorisations for everyone in the company. These were all signed off by the contracting officer, but as they knew there were staff rotations on site they never really kept track of the letters of authorisation you submitted. Most of the contracting officers were supportive of the security companies anyhow, and appreciated the work we did.

The Department of Defense badge was critically important. It meant you could eat in any DFAC in Iraq and had access to enter any base or clear any checkpoint. It also meant you were covered by the US military insurance under the Defense Base Act, which was cheaper than any of the private insurance companies, and their payouts were a lot better. The premiums were paid annually by the company for its members.

Payment for a project was simple. The security provider would invoice the construction company monthly. The construction company – as the prime contractor – would invoice the US government, including our invoice. All contracts were on a cost-plus basis. In many instances this meant the prime contractor added 20% to our invoice as a standard mark-up on every invoice.

Clearly this was a dubious way of handling payments, as the system was rigged against the government. It was hardly in the best interests of the prime contractor to save costs, as this meant that their mark-up profit would decrease. In fact, the more they spent, the more money they made. This model never really changed until 2010 in Afghanistan – that was how long it took for the US to figure out that the contracting system they were using was stacked against them.

As an example of the sort of monies involved, between 2004 and 2008 we were billing over a million dollars for a large site. Security profit margins were about 40%. Of course, if the equipment had already been paid for on a previous site then the margin increased. In short, what this meant was that the US government could pay up to ten times for the same equipment because every new project billed for the equipment and mobilisation costs. The biggest cost item then and now was armoured vehicles.

Payments were different for the various contracts. The government often paid biweekly. In these instances, invoices had to be submitted electronically to the contracting officer for authorisation. Another method was for monthly or scheduled payments linked to the work in progress on the site.

Working with a prime contractor meant that they paid you, and often the payment agreement would be 60 to 90 days. In the early days, most of the security companies could not afford to carry this expense for three months, as it could amount to hundreds of thousands of dollars. This forced many companies to factorise their invoices.

Simply put, this meant selling accounts receivable to a financial institution or investor – known as a factor. While factoring has been around for hundreds of years, it is now outdated as financing costs can easily exceed 20% of the value of the receivables.

I realised that we would have to use this process of factoring. In 2004 our factoring costs were 5% of the invoice submitted. But then payment would take only a week, and there were benefits as we would not have to waste time chasing money. The downside was that, on a million dollars, 5% was a lot of money to lose.

All the factoring companies were American, and were directly linked to the company issuing the invoice. This meant that the factoring company knew they would be paid, and in many instances the construction company would tell you what factoring company to use for their invoices.

In the difficult business world of Iraq, factoring was essential, but it was costly and would eventually be one of the main reasons for the break-up of our company in 2009.

8
A day in the Green Zone

After our day in the Green Zone we headed back to the Al Hamra, stopping to buy a chicken for supper. It was a beautiful night, and after we'd eaten we sat beside the pool to drink coffee.

Sitting alone at a table was a new guy.

'Mind if we join you?' I asked.

'Sure, pull up some chairs,' he said. By his accent he was American.

It turned out he was the security manager of a construction company called Environmental Chemical Corp (ECC) and had just arrived in the country. He was staying at the Little Flowers Hotel next door.

'My company's looking for contracts here,' he said, adding that he'd met Mauritz and learnt about our company from him. 'We've done a lot of government work back in America but, you know, Iraq offers opportunities.'

'Your PSD team's the French guys?' I said, half question, half statement.

'Sure is. We're using two teams currently. But we're on a low budget. Don't want to spend too much money until we've landed a contract. Problem is, we're having a job getting into the Green Zone. Nobody's got the right badges.'

'We've got badges,' I said. 'We could help out. Just let us know.'

Not long after that we said good night. Little did we know how that chat would pay off one day.

The next morning we were in the Green Zone early to attend the briefing by the Regional Security Officer. But our intention was also to breakfast there as we had not eaten bacon since leaving South Africa. I ate a double helping of bacon, three eggs and some chips – undoubtedly the best breakfast I'd had in Iraq.

By the time we got to the briefing room it was packed with security personnel, including some South African companies. We recognised Marius van der Riet, owner of Reed Inc, now living in the US but once in the SADF's intelligence section. Reed Inc we knew was mainly a logistics company, using their own security to protect their convoys. There was also Meteoric Tactical Solutions, who were running a few contracts looking after diplomats in Baghdad. They were the most successful South African crew, owned by Festus van Rooyen, Harry Carlse and Louwtjie Horn, ex-Special Forces and police task force. (Carlse and Horn would be arrested in Zimbabwe in March 2004 as part of the Simon Mann-led contingent planning a coup in Equatorial Guinea.) There were a few other South Africans, also ex-Special Forces and task force, working for foreign security companies – in total about ten.

The briefing was informative, giving a full intelligence picture for Baghdad and the surrounding area. This was our first overall assessment of the situation, and from the statistics things looked to be getting worse, not better. There were plenty of attacks on convoys.

After the briefing I met with Laurence Peters from the Private Security Company Association. The association kept a record of all the security companies operating in the country and sent out emails informing the companies of meetings and regulations that affected the private security industry. He would also get us listed as a security provider. Things were getting better by the minute.

I found the guys in the dining area having a South African reunion. Not impossible to manage a second helping of bacon, I decided, and sat down with a bacon burger and coffee. The coffee was nice and strong and the milk was fresh.

We learnt a lot sitting there chatting. We also impressed the guys with our temporary passes – nobody had heard of them – although I sensed a distinct dislike for the Blackwater people who had organised them for us.

One thing that puzzled me was that everyone else, except us, was tooled up. 'What's with the guns and body armour?' I asked. 'This is the Green Zone. No problems here.'

'Ja, boet, you think, hey? This is a magnet for anybody with a mortar or missile to shoot. You hear the siren you put on your body armour and run for the nearest bunker.'

Everyone had their weapons with them because guns could not be left in the vehicles. At the security checkpoints they had to unload, and the weapons were on stage one in the buildings. Stage one meant no round in the chamber, no magazine, the hammer forward and the weapon on safe.

We chatted on about our hotels and where to buy equipment, about friends and colleagues from our army days. I realised that most of the companies were made up of guys who knew one another. It was a close network of trust and recommendation. If you were unknown you weren't going to get hired. This made sense, as a contract depended on the quality of the staff, and our lives depended on those working with us.

One of the pressing issues nagging at me was how these guys were getting in and out of the country. It turned out that most of them were on US government contracts and used the military flights from Kuwait. Meteoric Tactical Solutions were using the route through Jordan and a flight from Amman to Dubai then to Johannesburg.

'But you need a visa to get out of the airport and that's impossible,' we were told.

Years later, we would find a loophole in this system. Today, of course, if you fly Emirates you can get a visa through them, and if you have more than an eight-hour wait for an onward flight they will arrange a hotel room. In the early 2000s things were very different.

'But now, listen,' I said, 'where are you guys getting weapons?'

'From the gun smugglers,' I was told.

The gun smugglers were mostly out in the tribal lands and had got their hands on military or police weapons after the war. Some of them were military officers who'd seen an opportunity to make a quick buck. There were lots of people looking for weapons: not only the security companies but the enemy as well. Payment was in cash, but you had to be sure that what you were buying was in good condition. Often it wasn't. In those days an AK-47 cost about $700 with seven magazines. A PKM machine gun was about $1 000. Ammunition prices fluctuated, but you could work on 50 cents a round and a dollar for the PKM.

This world of arms smugglers was new to us. We didn't always do things by the book but sometimes you had to go over to the dark side. We'd soon have plenty of experience with shady types, and this would stand us in good stead in Afghanistan in the years to come.

Later on, we'd buy weapons from people who had been contracted by the US Army to destroy them. But why destroy something you can sell for a profit? These people were easier to deal with and the quality of the hardware was better. Buying weapons out of a parking lot, as we had been doing, meant you had no opportunity to test them. The result was that we ended up with some duds, but that meant we had plenty of spare parts to repair any damaged weapons.

Our conversation with our fellow South Africans drifted through the morning into lunch. As we queued up to be served we were talking in Afrikaans when a young woman turned to me and said we should be careful what we said.

'There are lots of troops from Denmark here,' she said. 'They can understand what you're saying.'

Not sure that I could understand Danish, but it was a lesson learnt and a friend made. It turned out that she worked in the contracting department of the US military, based in the embassy, and had handled many of the contracts that had been outsourced to the Danes. It was more relief work than anything else, and nothing on the scale of the work being handled by Americans, but she was an important 'in' to the system.

Through her we were introduced to the United Nations security advisor, also stationed at the embassy. They had served in the army together. From him we learnt that the UN had withdrawn from Iraq after their compound was bombed in August 2003. Fourteen officials had been killed and more than a hundred wounded when a cement truck laden with explosives was driven through the security wall and detonated. They were now working their Iraq services out of Amman in Jordan.

'If you need any support, contact us,' he said. 'The chief of security in Amman is also a South African.'

It seemed we were everywhere.

I was sitting there enjoying my really good hamburger and chips when I heard some soldiers at a nearby table complaining about how bad the food was compared to other bases. Even inside the Green Zone they said there were other dining rooms serving better food. I couldn't believe them. As far as I was concerned, meals didn't get any better.

After lunch we headed to the supply store, hoping to buy steaks and groceries, but the fridges were empty. Another company was having a braai and had purchased all the meat. We browsed the equipment shelves and bought a couple of knives that would be handy additions to our grab bags.

As we were leaving, Rieme bumped into one of his old Recce buddies. He was working for a company called Olive out of a villa in the Green Zone. They were the ones having a braai and invited us to join them the following Friday.

'No, man, you guys must come,' he said. 'There's a nice bar, it's a great place.'

We assured him we'd be there.

Their party that night was for clients, and they used the Friday braai as a marketing tactic for old and new clients.

'The people at Olive have got it taped,' he assured us.

In later years, these parties became critical for business in the Green Zone and companies would spend thousands of dollars on entertainment to attract clients. If you were in the market for security, life in Baghdad could be an endless series of parties.

However, we didn't go this route and only on the odd occasion did we invite clients round to a party at one of our villas.

While we'd been enjoying the food and camaraderie in the

Green Zone, Hassan had found a taxi company prepared to rent out vehicles and drivers for missions in and around Baghdad.

The next morning, half an hour ahead of schedule, a driver arrived who spoke fairly good English. I was as impressed with his punctuality as I was with his carefully maintained GMC SUV (GMC is a division of General Motors), which had a full tank of fuel.

'Can you take us to the Ministry of Electricity?' I asked.

'No problem,' he said. 'But I do not have the right documents to enter there.'

'That's okay,' I reassured him, 'we just want to see where the place is.'

This brought a puzzled frown to his face but he shrugged and said, of course, we could go.

Being out in a taxi meant we'd be low profile, but we weren't taking chances. We dressed in T-shirts, body armour and then a shirt over the body armour to disguise it. We also wore *shemagh*s, the black checked scarves that Iraqis wore.

Our weapons – the small MP5s – were in our tog bags, and we had extra magazines in our grab bags. I sat up front, Rieme and Snoeks in the middle and Eddie and Hassan at the back.

As we drove along it was obvious that no one gave us a second glance. We were invisible, just a part of the traffic flow. It was a very different experience to being in the Nissan Patrols, which seemed to draw attention.

A high-profile PSD team came past and forced us off the road, which pissed me off.

'Look at them,' I gesticulated. 'The arseholes.' The rear gunner was waving his fist and threatening everyone with his weapon.

Two of our team members in thawbs, *the white garments worn by many Arab men, and* shemaghs *(Arab headdress). While the* shemagh *was worn throughout the country, the* thawb *differed between provinces.*

I reckon it was on that mission that the concept of the low-profile PSD team was really born for OSSI/Safenet. It was how we had operated in the military and it was how we were going to operate now. In our army days we'd painted ourselves black, worn wigs and used the equipment the insurgents used. Nothing had changed. If our clients were anonymous, no one was going to shoot at them. We'd look like every other car on the road.

The high-profile tactic was to form a 'bubble' of security around the convoy. And to maintain this at all costs. That meant driving fast in armoured vehicles, and being aggressive. We would be in normal 'soft skin' sedans and SUVs, although we did modify them to allow us a little more protection. The benefit of the soft skin was that you could immediately lay down accurate fire on the enemy, which gave you an advantage in a firefight. For one thing, you could shoot out of the windows, whereas in armoured vehicles you couldn't open the windows and very few of the vehicles had gun ports. And then our gunner with his machine gun couldn't be seen by the insurgents because the rear windows were tinted. This added to the element of surprise. In later years, turrets were added to the armoured vehicles.

Our taxi mission went well, in fact better than anticipated. A client plus one of us for protection would be perfectly safe in a taxi. With extra shemaghs to disguise clients we'd be ahead of the game. These shemaghs – worn mostly as protection against the sun and dust – were patterned in different colours according to tribal custom. In Baghdad they were mostly red and white check or black and white check. We acquired six checked and a plain black one in case there was a woman in the group.

If there was a downside to the taxis it came when getting out of the vehicle. With only one protection officer, there was a higher level of exposure, but we decided we would just have to make it work.

As a contingency, we came to an arrangement with the guards at the hotel that we could hire their off-duty staff if we needed more manpower. We also prepared extra medical bags that we would use in the vehicles when we had the clients with us. At night we would leave them in the clients' rooms.

Our intention was to keep our weapons concealed and to make do without sunglasses, as none of the locals wore them. Locals also drove with their windows open. As we were at the tail end of winter and the weather was still cool this was no problem, but I knew that in summer it would be an entirely different matter. Fortunately the GMC had a separate aircon system for the back of the vehicle that could be switched on when we were transporting clients.

One of the vehicles we used when we travelled low-profile.

Another advantage was the curtains that taxis had fitted to the rear windows. Mostly these were to protect passengers from the sun on long trips to the border but they were used in the city as well.

All we needed now were the clients.

9
The Kuwait misadventure

In February 2004 the search for clients took Mauritz and John to Kuwait. Getting to the Kuwaiti border was a long 700-km drive to the southeast of the country. Clearly this was not a mission we could do in a day, but we could get our bosses to the Umm Qasr border crossing if we left early enough from Baghdad.

On the return run, the most logical place to overnight was Basra. We didn't know the route, so we had no idea where fuel would be available. But fortunately we had Hassan, who knew Basra, and a hotel that had secure parking for the vehicles. He'd also been to the border post, so we were not travelling entirely blind.

Apart from fuel, the only other problem I could foresee was coming up behind a slow American convoy. This was a major route for American supplies into Iraq and was therefore a targeted route for IED detonations.

Getting out of Baghdad was slower than we'd anticipated because of all the checkpoints in the first hundred kilometres. We had allowed for this and weren't too concerned as the border post was open at night to facilitate the movement of the US convoys.

About halfway to the border we came across a fuel point and decided to fill the tanks. There was a little shop nearby and Mauritz bought stocks of chips, soft drinks and two cartons of cigarettes.

'What the hell d'you want cigarettes for?' I asked. 'You started smoking?'

'No, man, they're for the border. I heard they can be useful. You never know, we might need them.'

I had no idea why we would need to bribe the customs officials at the border post but Mauritz was often off on his own mission, so I didn't question him any further.

All along the route we were reminded of the hostile activities that rendered this road unsafe. There were burnt-out trucks, the wrecks of vehicles, the remains of IEDs that had exploded as the convoys came thundering past.

'Bloody glad we don't do any escorting along this stretch,' I said to Mauritz. Because, looking at the aftermath, sooner or later you were going to be attacked.

We were in low-profile mode at the time, without boards on the front and back of our Nissan Patrols to warn other road users away. We wore shemaghs and jackets over our body armour. At a quick glance we would pass for Iraqis.

We made it to Basra without incident and quickly noticed the difference between this city – which was under the control of the British – and Baghdad. Here the British undertook both vehicle and foot patrols, and the city felt a lot safer. Of course, Baghdad was much bigger, but the contrast was noticeable. My belief was that foot patrols meant that the locals and the soldiers had a chance to communicate with one another. It was critical that the troops didn't reckon on every Iraqi being an insurgent. Also the population would then see that the troops were not there to kill them but to protect them.

We were soon through Basra, and the short distance to the border crossing went quickly enough. I was surprised to see that the Iraqi border post consisted of a collection of mobile homes.

We stopped in the parking area and Mauritz and John went

to clear themselves through the Iraq customs, with Hassan and Rieme tagging along. The rest of us stayed in the vehicles. Walking around with guns was hardly a good idea; besides, the PKM machine gun couldn't be stowed in a bag.

At one point I saw Mauritz return and collect his cartons of cigarettes, and this should have raised a red flag but I let it pass.

It was not long before they were all back.

'What's the scene?' I asked.

'I've organised everything with the captain,' said Mauritz, clearly pleased with himself. 'You can drive us across the no-man's-land and drop us at the Kuwait side. We'll get our passports stamped and then catch the bus to Kuwait City.'

'This isn't a good idea.'

'It'll be fine,' said Mauritz.

I had my doubts.

The Iraqi captain duly waved us through and we drove slowly across no-man's-land, stopping on the Kuwait side in front of their checkpoint building. We all got out of the vehicles to say goodbye to John and Mauritz. We took off our body armour and put the weapons aside. I could see that we were getting strange glances from the Kuwait military and this made me edgy. Mauritz and John went inside to have their passports stamped, while we waited with their luggage. They appeared in the doorway, all smiles.

'Hey, Hassan, Eddie,' called out Mauritz, 'give us a hand with the bags, man.'

'They can't do that,' I shouted back.

'Ag, man, don't worry,' said Mauritz. 'Come'n bring the bags.'

'Don't,' I said to Hassan and Eddie.

'He's the boss,' said Eddie.

At the boom, the Kuwait military wanted all the passports. Of course Eddie's and Hassan's passports were in the vehicle. They were both immediately arrested and marched back to the vehicles to retrieve their passports.

I approached the captain and asked if I could resolve the issue.

'They have entered Kuwait without visas,' he said. 'Why have they come to Kuwait without visas?'

'They didn't know they would be entering Kuwait,' I explained.

'But there is the sign,' he said, pointing to a Welcome to Kuwait signboard. 'I have to arrest them. Why are they here with all these weapons? Are you going to attack Kuwait?'

I just knew there would be no easy resolution to this impasse.

He marched Eddie and Hassan into the office.

Outside, I could see Mauritz and John cheerfully waving goodbye as they climbed into the bus. I could equally cheerfully have killed them.

It took an hour and much talking and telephone conversations with the Iraqi captain to take the heat out of the situation. Eventually it was decided that if we paid a $500 spot fine they would release Hassan and Eddie. I paid the money and we were escorted back to the Iraqi side.

'Let's stop for a cup of coffee,' the guys said.

'No fucking way,' I replied. 'We'll stop in Basra. We've got no more money to waste on dumb ideas.'

Hassan looked completely distraught by the episode. I asked him if he was okay.

'I thought it was going to be very bad for me,' he said. 'The Kuwaitis hate us. If they put me in jail, you would never see me again. Iraqi people never come back from jails in Kuwait.'

This was the last time I ever wanted to go through a border crossing with Mauritz and John. I vowed never to get involved in Mauritz's little schemes again. If they had to fly via Miami to get to Kuwait, then so be it. I was not going through something like this again.

Famous last words, of course.

10
Down to business

Our first clients were part of an initiative by the US Army to acquaint American businesses with the programme for the reconstruction of Iraq. They were flown in by the military and given a week to set up meetings with local businessmen.

Our group was led by a woman called Stephanie Jasen and we were to meet them at the US embassy. But before that John and Mauritz were flying in to perform the necessary client liaison and to run the ops room. Having them in the ops room would allow us to concentrate on the missions that we anticipated would be daily and in different parts of the city and surroundings. And then we would need guards at night for the clients.

We repositioned in the vehicles for the trip to the Jordanian border with Snoeks and Rieme in the gunship and Eddie, Hassan and me in the lead Nissan Patrol. This was necessary because I was almost deaf in my left ear and could not hear Rieme if he spoke to me from the rear of the vehicle. My deafness had started back in Angola during the Border War when an RPG-7 exploded a little too close for comfort. But I had learnt to live with the deafness, and when there were three of us in the vehicle it was no problem.

The trip to the border was as tense as always, and there were more checkpoints in the triangle of death between Fallujah and Ramadi. There were terrorists hiding out in the area and there were reported to be training bases in the desert. There'd been a step-up in attacks, and this would escalate until the killing of the

Blackwater contractors in Fallujah in March, which precipitated the invasion of that city by the Americans in retaliation. (Four American contractors for Blackwater, who were doing a delivery for food caterers, were killed in an ambush by Iraqi insurgents. Their corpses were dragged through Fallujah and later hung from a bridge.)

Mauritz, as was becoming his custom, had brought three cold boxes of goodies for us. We loaded their luggage into the vehicles, John, as usual, travelling light. He was typical CIA. Everything had to be perfectly packed. Each non-clothing item was independently wrapped and sealed. It must have taken him hours to pack. Even his laptop was placed strategically so that it could be taken out easily at airport security points. His briefcase had to hang in a particular way over his main bag. I suppose this came from years of travel. He was easily disconcerted by delays and struggling travellers who might hold up the queue in front of him. For this reason he travelled business class to avoid the crowds.

We left the border after lunch and, despite the tension of being constantly alert, arrived in Baghdad that evening without a hitch. Having John in the lead vehicle meant that I could brief him on our strategies of using taxis and the low-profile approach. He was also quite impressed to hear that we had managed to get passes for the Green Zone.

I then got round to a pressing issue: money. I had a reserve fund of $2 000 for fuel and emergencies but that was our total cash in hand. We had to pay the hotel accounts, and hiring taxis was a daily cash expense of $800, or $150 per vehicle, fuel included. Which I thought fair. It was unlikely we'd get it any cheaper. But we needed more cash on a monthly basis, and I made this clear.

John listened to my accounting without comment.

That evening we ate in the dining hall so that he could brief us on the clients. There were six of them and they each had different itineraries. We booked six suites and arranged a schedule of 24-hour guards. All was set for our first contract. Mauritz also informed us that he had followed up on a lead of someone looking for protection on convoys taking scrap metal to Jordan.

The next day we collected our clients from the US embassy in two vehicles and assisted with their hotel check-in. We agreed on a two-hour rest and recuperation period, prior to a briefing at the pool. I took the first watch on their floor and put a chair at the end of the passage so I had a clear view and would notice any movement.

When we gathered at the pool later that day, we explained our low-profile approach using taxis and disguise. I marvelled at how relaxed everyone was. We handed out the shemaghs and demonstrated how they were to be worn. Stephanie was given a black scarf to cover her blonde hair.

'Just one other thing,' I said to end the briefing, 'if one of us gives an order, don't hesitate, just do what we say. We're here to protect you, but you must want to be protected as well.'

Then began five days of missions using the taxis. Each day there was huge potential for an incident. Each day I ticked off with relief when our clients closed their hotel doors.

The five days passed without any problems and the taxi system worked efficiently.

On the last night there was a dinner hosted by the Sandi and Dyncorp private military security companies. Stephanie had arranged the event. Dyncorp was a major player in Iraq at the time, and Sandi was one of their subcontractors on the

Iraqi police training programme. It was an important dinner for us and would have a marked influence on our business.

The venue was a restaurant, and we decided that one team would recce the site before the other group brought in the clients. Once there, we would enter the restaurant low-profile with our weapons in bags, and two guys would remain outside the building to protect the vehicles and ensure the area remained safe. We would then rotate so that everyone had an opportunity to eat. Our table was positioned with clear lines of sight to all the entrances and an unobstructed view of the clients.

The evening went uneventfully and the next morning we drove our clients back to the embassy at the end of their tour. Our first contract had been highly successful. In addition, it had given us valuable experience and shown that we worked as a team. But after five full days of working and guard duty at night, the hours were beginning to take their toll. We were all in need of rest, and took the next two days off.

I spent that time going over the accounts with John and Mauritz. I needed to keep them both happy, and to ensure that every cent was accounted for I had spreadsheets and all the signed-off receipts. Both men were worried that one might be putting in more capital than the other, which was why it was critical that I had up-to-date information. They wanted to know where every dollar went, and to this end grilled me over those two days. But in the end they were satisfied.

The fact that this client group brought in a little money made them open to my request for more money to pay the hotel and for working capital. My next task was to register the company with the Ministry of Trade.

One of the concerns with registering the company was a possible change of name. I thought we could go in as OSSI/Safenet and change the name if there were issues with the documentation of one of the companies. If anything, I expected there might be problem with Safenet, as there was no Iraqi embassy in South Africa. There was an embassy in America.

One afternoon Hassan and I met with a lawyer at the Al Hamra and he outlined all our potential expenses. His fee was $1 000 a month, the accountant would be about $10 000 a year, company tax would be a flat 5% of profit, and personal tax for any Iraqis in our employ would be $50 a year. Social security was 17% of the salary paid to the guard. Expats were exempt from tax. He stressed that the social security payments were important, as we had to have a letter of good standing each month from the Department of Social Security in order to renew the company licence.

I had letters appointing him and the accounting firm written in Arabic and printed out using the business centre at the nearby Flower Land Hotel. Hassan was good with computers and Microsoft Office and handled the whole transaction. In fact his computer skills would come in useful in the future.

Once all the paperwork was submitted, the lawyer reckoned it could take anything from two weeks to a month for the registration to come through. Nothing was computerised, everything had to be done by hand.

In the end it took three weeks. Armed with the licence I opened both dollar and dinar bank accounts. Internet banking had yet to come to Iraq so we needed cheques for local transactions, while international transfers were a nightmare. Iraq was not linked to the SWIFT code system, which meant that money had to be transferred via an intermediary bank in

Jordan. We used the Bank of Baghdad with Citibank in the US as the intermediary. A transfer from the US would take about three days, which wasn't bad going. Using any other bank would have taken about two weeks.

To pay for expensive items I soon found out that post-dated cheques were an acceptable way of doing business.

My next query to the bank was about running our payroll from the bank account.

'No, not possible,' Hassan told me. 'Iraqi men don't trust banks. They want cash. You see, they don't want their wives knowing how much money is in a bank account.'

This wasn't a problem but it was an inconvenience. I didn't want to handle large amounts of cash once we started employing locals. We would be transporting money to the sites, and this put us at risk. Not a comfortable situation, but there was no way round it.

While the company registration process was finalised, I started looking into the feasibility of hiring a villa. We couldn't stay at the hotel indefinitely as it was expensive, but I soon found out that hiring a villa was not all that easy either.

For one thing, if the villa was to be used as a business address the owner would be taxed accordingly. Of course he would pass this cost on to the renter. Then villas were rented on a yearly basis with six-month extensions if you were lucky. However, the rental had to be paid in advance in US dollars. In 2004, the price of a small villa of three to four bedrooms and bathrooms with a small garden and parking for a single vehicle was about $5 000 a month. In other words we'd have to put down $60 000. Even if it was furnished I calculated that additional basics might cost another $5 000.

The biggest expense in running a villa was the generator.

At the time, there were about five hours of power a day from the general grid, the rest you had to generate yourself. The unit would cost anything between $6 000 and $10 000 plus an automatic transfer switch, which added $2 000 to the bill. Diesel, difficult to buy and not readily available, averaged a dollar a litre and we would need tanks capable of holding at least 2 000 litres of fuel. On top of that, finding a mechanic to maintain and service the generator would not be an easy task.

All this had to be weighed against the costs and convenience of staying in the hotel. I would definitely miss the swimming pool. I had watched the temperature climb from 8^0C when we arrived to 14^0C now in February 2004. A degree or two more and I could start doing some serious swimming.

An opportunity to make a little money came up while we waited for the company to be registered. A security company called DA Vance needed a convoy protection team from the Jordanian border to Baghdad. They were working with John in Kurdistan and turned to him for help.

He signed us up.

We were familiar with the route, but as a precaution added a satellite phone to our equipment. It was also the only way to keep in contact with DA Vance in Baghdad and John in the US.

To collect the first convoy, we left Baghdad at midnight and arrived at the border at first light. Our outward plan was to refuel at Fallujah and then again at the border if we could. If there was no fuel at the border it wasn't that much of a problem as we knew we had the range to make it back to the city.

Travelling at night was also in our favour because the

possibility of insurgents, triggering IEDs was very low. We made good time, but the convoy we were due to meet was delayed and only arrived at midday.

I was not happy and let DA Vance know that this was not part of our plan. We'd agreed to meet the convoy at seven in the morning in order to be in Baghdad by nightfall.

'We'll update you at noon,' the DA Vance operator informed me.

We listlessly passed the hours, ate our normal chicken lunch, and watched midday come and go.

I put through another call to DA Vance.

'So where are they?' I asked.

'They're at the border. But there's some delay,' I was told. 'Maybe two hours more.'

'Any later than that and we have to wait until tomorrow,' I said.

That meant we'd be sleeping in the vehicles, as there were no hotels near this border crossing.

By two o'clock there was still no sign of the trucks.

Again a call to DA Vance. 'The trucks are crossing now,' was their response.

We checked. Even got permission to cross the border to see if our trucks were waiting to be processed. There was a long queue of trucks on the Jordanian side but the ones we were waiting for were not among them.

Back on the Iraqi side I phoned again.

'The trucks are there. They will be crossing soon,' the DA Vance operator said.

'Hogwash,' I replied. 'We've checked all the trucks on both sides of the border. They're not there. We're leaving. If you get a reliable update we'll come back and escort them.'

Then John phoned. 'Listen, Neil,' he said. 'They've been delayed. They'll be at the border by five o'clock. Please stay on. These trucks are critical and could lead to more work for us.'

Staying on was the last thing I wanted to do. And the team was just as unhappy. If there was a plus factor it was that moving the trucks at night would be safer than during the day.

By four there was still no sign of the trucks.

I decided that five o'clock would be our cut-off point.

At five I phoned DA Vance to tell them we were returning to Baghdad without the convoy.

I was pissed off, we were all pissed off. We'd wanted to do the mission and had now wasted a day cooling our heels.

About an hour from the border, John rang.

'The trucks are at the border,' he said. 'They're waiting for you.'

'Tell them to come on,' I said. 'We'll wait for them at the first fuel stop.' It was a landmark they couldn't miss.

'Okay, sure' he said. 'It doesn't make sense for you guys to drive back. I'll tell them.'

By ten that night there was still no sign of the trucks.

This time a call to DA Vance produced a different story.

'Sorry, guys,' we were told. 'We've been lied to. The trucks haven't left Amman yet. There was something wrong with the paperwork.'

We decided to sleep where we were. I phoned John to let him know and said that if the trucks were ready the next day we'd be there to collect them.

'It is not a good idea to sleep here,' Hassan said. 'This is when the terrorists move about. They will find us. Also there are smugglers. They bring alcohol and cigarettes and they are even better armed than the terrorists. They kill people so that they are not identified. And it is very cold.'

True on all counts. It was still winter and the nights were bitterly cold. No possibility of running the engines to keep the heaters going either, as we would run out of fuel.

'Grin and bear it, guys,' I said.

We positioned the vehicles behind a wall so that they were not visible from the road but we still had sight of the road. Then we assigned guard duty. We would work in pairs, with one guy outside the vehicle who would hear any movement and would do regular patrols of the fuel stop.

Rieme and I drew the early-morning shift from one to five. We were sitting on the ground next to the vehicles when I heard movement.

The moon was out so we could see fairly well.

I signalled to Rieme the direction I'd heard the noise.

He indicated that he'd heard it too.

We slipped off the safety catches on our weapons and prepared to fire. I was sure we were about to be attacked.

We had some cover and at least we were prepared.

The noise came again.

'Sounds like a dog,' Rieme whispered.

Not one dog but a pack of dogs. Wild dogs in the middle of the desert? No sign of humans for miles: what did these dogs live on?

We grinned at one another in relief.

The next morning we breakfasted on snacks we'd bought at the border the previous day. A cup of coffee would have been welcome but there was no chance of that until Baghdad.

By seven o'clock we were on the road, convinced that the mission would not be happening. The drive was easy and uneventful although there many more burnt-out trucks along the side of the road than there had been on the outward trip.

'These are not done by terrorists,' Hassan said. 'These are local people. When the trucks are without an escort they stop them to steal the load. Then they set them on fire. Probably they kill the driver.'

Probably they kill the driver – a reminder, if we needed it, that we lived in desperate times in a desperate country.

11
The scrap metal convoy

About this time, Mauritz's Jordanian connection asked for a meeting at the Hunting Club in Baghdad. The contract would involve escorting scrap metal trucks to the border with Jordan. We were about to experience the dark side of the PSD business.

The Hunting Club had a reputation in the city as the elite club of the rich and powerful. In its heyday it had been frequented by Saddam Hussein and had then featured a racetrack, which had subsequently been redeveloped as gardens for the big mosque Saddam was building on the site. The restaurant was still in operation and supported by the city's top-drawer businessmen. We looked forward to lunching at the Hunting Club.

The restaurant had all the trappings of an exclusive establishment, with discreet but firm security. We had to phone our potential clients in order to gain entrance.

Before lunch we discussed business in a small conference room. The Jordanian told us he had almost concluded the deal with the Iraqi government and was waiting for the go-ahead. His company would be cutting up and removing all the destroyed military hardware – tanks, other vehicles, even damaged artillery pieces – left after the war. We would then escort the scrap metal to the border with Jordan. There were two 'graveyards' where the dismantling would occur: one outside Baghdad, the other near Fallujah. His intention was to keep the trucks rolling constantly.

Mauritz had a few conditions. Each mission would be cash upfront. We would not escort more than five trucks at a time and if one broke down it would be left behind. All trucks had to be full of fuel before departure or we wouldn't leave. He advised the Jordanian to have an extra horse in the convoy so that if a truck broke down the trailer could be hitched up and continue to the border. Nobody would want to be at the whims of fate on the road between Fallujah and Ramadi. The client asked if he could accompany the first mission, and no one objected.

Lunch was next on the agenda. We all ordered steak, which was excellent.

As we left, I asked if we could visit the two 'graveyards' so that we could plan the mission in detail.

'That is a good idea,' he said, shaking our hands at the entrance to the club.

We walked in silence to our vehicles.

'I don't know, Mauritz,' I said, 'I don't trust this guy. Just as well you told him cash upfront.'

Behind us I heard murmurs of agreement from the other guys.

'He's too smooth,' said Hassan. 'I don't trust him either.'

'He's well connected,' said Mauritz. 'Right up there with the high-ranking officials. And I know he's got the financial backing.'

That might be so, but something did not seem right. Why would he need a PSD team to escort his trucks to the border? Why would anybody want to steal scrap metal? It was no use to anyone, and certainly not the insurgents. My feeling was that the Jordanian was using the escort to get through the checkpoints without any holdups. When he got to the border, if he didn't have the correct paperwork that was his problem. At $8 000 a convoy, this was not bad money for us and would pay the bills if we could do two or three runs a month.

We visited the Baghdad 'graveyard' and I was pleased to see that there were five teams wielding blowtorches and angle grinders, working a yard that must have been a square kilometre in size. That was a lot of scrap to cut. The manager reckoned that it would be another week before they started to load the trucks.

Back at the Al Hamra I assured Mauritz that the project seemed legitimate enough.

'Just as well,' he said, 'money's tight, we need a cash injection.'

About a week later the Jordanian met us at the hotel with the news that trucks would be loaded by the end of the next day.

'Fine,' said Mauritz. 'All okay. Just one matter outstanding.'

The Jordanian pulled out an envelope. 'Please check the money,' he said.

'I'm sure it's all there,' Mauritz replied, weighing the packet in his hand. But the Jordanian was hardly out the door before he started counting the bills.

We were well prepared for the mission. We put radios in each of the trucks so that Hassan had communication with them. Eddie and I were in the lead vehicle, with Rieme, Snoeks and Hassan at the back. Once the trucks were at the border post our job was over and we could return to Baghdad. Mauritz was in the ops room and we would let him know arrival and departure times by satellite phone.

The truck drivers had been briefed in the use of the radios and told to stay two truck lengths apart at a speed of 110 km/h. None of them wanted to be bypassing Fallujah too slowly. As they approached the border they would bunch up so that they could go through the checkpoint as an identifiable convoy.

We had decided that our vehicles would be low-profile with no tell-tale signs at the rear warning other road users to stay back. I had no intention of making it easy for terrorists to identify us.

At the first checkpoint, the marines warned us that a convoy had been hit during the night near the Jordanian border. Good luck, they said, and kindly radioed ahead to the other checkpoints to let them know we were bringing a five-truck convoy through.

In those days there were no clearances required, and you did not have to notify the authorities of your movements. All this would change dramatically in the coming months.

I had the client with us in the vehicle and could see his relief as we pulled out of the checkpoint.

'Were you worried?' I asked.

'In the times before today the Americans have held up my trucks for three days,' he said. 'They said the paperwork was not correct.'

This was news to me; certainly he'd never mentioned it during our meetings. Back came that feeling that something wasn't right. If his paperwork wasn't legitimate, how did he expect to get through first the Iraqi and then the Jordanian border posts?

At the border there was a change of plan. The client now wanted to be taken to the captain in charge of customs.

'I don't like plans that change,' I told him.

'Don't worry. It will not take long,' he replied.

The captain was an obliging man and asked us to wait in the dining room while he met with our client.

'Doesn't want us to see money changing hands,' Rieme said to me in Afrikaans.

Perhaps he was right. The meeting lasted a mere five minutes. We were then invited to a lunch of fried eggs and chips with fresh bread served on well-worn plastic plates.

'It is a meal you cannot refuse,' our client pointed out.

We were hardly going to refuse food. Besides, sharing a meal was an important social event and showed respect for the visitor. No matter how poor the host might be, he would put whatever he had on the table to honour his guests.

There was no cutlery and Hassan whispered to me that I would have to eat traditional-style with my right-hand fingers and use the bread to mop up. This was tricky. And messy. Eventually I resorted to my Leatherman to cut up the egg, which brought a smile to the captain's face. In time we would become skilled in this way of eating. As always, the meal ended with a cup of chai.

The next part of the process was to get through the border. There was a queue of trucks at least 50 vehicles long both leaving Iraq and waiting to enter Jordan. I could foresee this taking hours. But the client had the papers for his trucks cleared in ten minutes and then went over to the Jordanian side to expedite matters there. Another ten minutes and he assured us that everything was in order.

At first he asked us to approach the Jordanians but I wanted as little to do with his operation as possible and insisted that he handle the paperwork. I was sure this was a dodgy deal, and certainly jumping the queue proved the point.

We drove back to Baghdad without incident, the client sleeping the whole way. When we parted, he was effusive with praise and thanks, reminding me that each time we delivered a convoy to the border post we should see the captain.

Surely these guys were stealing the scrap metal from the government? Hassan backed my suspicions, adding that there must be some powerful people involved or they wouldn't be able to carry it off so openly.

I took our concerns to Mauritz. He was blunt. Without this we would have to close down. Expenses were close to R250 000 a month. If this could be offset against an income of between $20 000 to $40 000 for the convoys then that would buy us time to land a decent contract.

'When that happens I'll pull the plug on these missions,' he promised.

Mauritz and John had gambled everything on getting this venture off the ground and there was a very good chance they would lose everything if we didn't land a contract soon.

We did a number of these missions during March, and each one went smoothly. Then the second 'graveyard' south of Fallujah came on stream and the client informed us that trucks would now be leaving from there as well. Using Google Earth we established that we would have to drive through the centre of Fallujah.

'No,' said Hassan. 'This is impossible. It is too dangerous.'

'We've got no other options,' I replied. 'We're just going to have to plan it really well.' All we could do was try and reduce the risk. Hassan wasn't the only one concerned about the danger; we all were.

The client let us know that the first mission from Fallujah would be on the last day of March. Mauritz was in South Africa and I was handling the financial side.

THE SCRAP METAL CONVOY

'That's okay,' I said. 'But we need the money first or no mission.'

Yes, yes, I was reassured the money would be there as normal.

But, the day before, the client arrived at the hotel without all the money. He would make a down payment of half and with the next mission pay the remainder.

Two things worried me about this, the half payment being the first. Then I suspected that, as there were no major checkpoints from Fallujah to the border, bar the one at Ramadi, and as his trucks were now easily recognised by the marines, he was intending to dump us. We were little more than insurance, and maybe he thought he could do without the insurance?

'All the money or no mission,' I told him.

'Then I will pay the day after the mission,' he said.

'We will delay for a day until you make the payment.' I was not going to budge.

He threatened and cajoled, saying that if we did not do this mission we would get no more work from him.

'That's fine,' I said. 'You're the one breaking the agreement.'

He stormed off in a fury.

'He is saving face,' explained Hassan. 'We will see.'

As I had no intention of chasing money, I told the team the mission was off. We'd never felt good about the Fallujah run so this came as a relief to all of us.

The next morning, at the briefing in the Green Zone, we learnt that four Americans had been killed in an ambush in Fallujah the previous day and their bodies hung from a bridge. They were Blackwater personnel – Scott Helvenston, Jerry Zovko, Wesley Batalona and Mike Teague. The ambush had occurred in the city and we would have driven right into it. It could have been us. That incident was to change many things.

12

First major contract

Two Americans that Eddie and I had befriended were advisors to the Ministry of Public Works and their job was to ensure that American interests were given top priority. They'd been in Iraq a while, worked out of the embassy and knew the ropes. Stephanie Jasen was linked to them as well. They had a security contract in the offing but said that unfortunately it had to go to an American company. No problem, I said, and we explained how OSSI/Safenet was part American with a US war veteran and former CIA officer as its founder-owner. They were immediately interested to meet with John and, as he was due in a few days, we set up a meeting.

'It's not a big contract, you understand,' the younger of the two men, Rick Clay, emphasised. He was tall with long, black, curly hair and a firm handshake. 'We just need security at the damaged Iraqi Air Force base, Al Muthenna.'

'Doesn't matter,' I said. 'We're up for it.'

Getting a contract such as the one they had pending would mean that we'd not only have the embassy badge but a DoD badge as well. This would be a game-changer for us.

John and Eddie met with Rick and his boss – a dead ringer for a dapper grandfather – while I waited in the DFAC dining room. We'd lunched there, as John had a hankering for their food, particularly the ice cream.

'You sure you guys've got this right?' he asked, sceptical that Eddie and I could have established good friends and contacts among the Americans.

FIRST MAJOR CONTRACT

'You'll see,' I reassured him.

And now here he was walking towards me, grinning broadly. He couldn't stop talking about the prospects; in fact I had not seen him so excited before. That Eddie had made the introductions was ignored: this was John's find and his contract, and all he needed now was a proposal.

Eddie smiled at me. He didn't need to say anything. Welcome to the business world.

I emailed Mauritz and updated him about what had transpired. By return I received a mail that he was on his way.

That evening we sat with John, working on the proposal. It was clear that we needed a site visit before we got down to details. We'd all driven past the Al Muthenna airfield and noted that many, if not most, of the buildings had been partially destroyed in the invasion.

The next day Rick Clay and his boss joined us at the site. We'd suggested they join us. Partly this was to deepen our relationship; partly it was a PR exercise to show them we were genuine.

At the gate was a marine sergeant who had been alerted to our pending arrival and was to act as our guide. He took us to two hangars where Rick and his boss were waiting. Rick wanted to show us the inside of the hangars so that we would know what we would be protecting.

'After seeing this, you might want to change how many men you use,' he said before the marines opened the hangars just wide enough for us to fit through.

I couldn't believe my eyes. The hangars were packed to the ceiling with Saddam Hussein's Iraqi dinars! There must have been trillions of dollars worth of cash in the building. The second hangar had the same amount of money.

Clearly, this was why they didn't want the local national guards on duty.

The money was due to be destroyed but was waiting for the US Department of State to organise the operation. How long this was going to take was anyone's guess.

Our main area of operation was to be the construction site of the Al-Rahman mosque that Saddam Hussein had been building on an adjacent site. We were to ensure that the theft of building materials and cranes stopped. Apparently tons of rebar had already been stolen and one of the big cranes had disappeared overnight. Our proposal, Rick emphasised, was not to mention the stockpiles of dinars.

The Al-Rahman mosque in central Baghdad.

We spent the next couple of hours surveying the site. There was a T-wall round much of the perimeter but some stretches were wire fencing which offered no security at all. This needed attention, and we would have to rebuild and repair some of

FIRST MAJOR CONTRACT

the buildings in order to have on-site accommodation. I did not want our staff living out of containers as they afforded no protection. In a firefight, what chance did you stand in a metal container?

Apart from the construction work that had to be done on the site, we would have to increase our staff contingent. These men had to be South Africans and they should have some sort of uniform, body armour, sleeping bags and radios, as well as night-vision binoculars. We also had to ensure we had enough medical equipment, insurance cover and contracts of service.

The contracts were for three months service in-country and then 28 days' paid leave at home, which meant accounting for home flights and leave rotations. The average salary was $9 000. On top of that was the insurance at 10% of the annual salary that had to be paid in advance. We also took out kidnap and ransom insurance on each member. We estimated a contingent of 40 operatives who would each require a $500 advance – called an 'in-country payment' – to buy cigarettes and other personal items when they arrived. Just the salary payroll alone was a hefty amount.

We contacted gunrunners to get the prices of AK-47s with seven loaded magazines, as well as five PKM machine guns with 800 rounds belted ammunition. Also, I wanted a price on five extra cases of AK and PKM ammunition.

In addition there were big-ticket items to purchase, such as a generator along with electrical cables, distribution boxes and an automatic transfer box so that the generator could be started remotely. And then there was a matter of provisions: groceries, bread, water.

Our proposal came in at $3,4 million, which included a profit. At first glance that might seem a hefty price tag, but in those days it was small change. We had already been offered salaries of $25 000 a month to work for other companies, but our loyalty was to Mauritz and John. If we left them, they would have no chance of getting up and running and would lose all their capital.

We submitted the proposal and were told that it would take about two weeks to get the funds cleared. This was a contract issued through the Iraqi government – which had been established on 20 April 2004 – supported by the US Department of State. If we got the contract I knew there would be an initial payment of what was termed 'mobilisation money' so that we could get our side operational.

By now John had returned to the US and Mauritz had arrived. I spent hours explaining the pricing to him and then set up a meeting with Rick and his boss at the embassy. We arranged a temporary pass for Mauritz, but when we arrived at the embassy that day, our contact at the Regional Security Officer's office told us he'd be rotating out in two weeks' time. He warned us that we'd have to make a plan with our temporary passes as he wouldn't be able to help us any longer and he didn't know who would replace him.

At the meeting with Rick and his boss, Mauritz was in his element. Mauritz had a natural salesman's instinct to charm his clients. He could sell ice to an Eskimo and the Eskimo would be convinced he'd got a good deal. However, I could see there was something bothering Rick. It soon came out that the price was too high. He reckoned he could get us $3,2 million at a push but that we'd have to trim the budget.

'The only way we can do that is to reduce the number of guards,' I said.

'You'll have to look elsewhere to make savings,' he responded.

FIRST MAJOR CONTRACT

'We're happy with the technical security plan and the personnel allocation.'

That meant we'd have to trim the profit margins.

'We'll make the cut,' said Mauritz. 'When do you want the new proposal?'

'Tonight,' said Rick.

'No problem,' said Mauritz.

This was tight. But Mauritz sat there for the rest of the lunch chatting amiably and really charming the clients. I could tell he was making a good impression.

We spent what was left of the afternoon trimming the budget by the required $200 000. In the end we dispensed with the second generator and did without other items without having to lessen the profit margin.

But even this wasn't enough. Rick came back to us with the news that unless we could come in at $3 million the contract would have to go to tender. We went back to the drawing board. Mauritz's attitude was that even if we broke even, this contract would open doors. We would have the badges we needed, we would have access to the military hospitals, and we would be seen as competitive with the other security companies.

As a result, out went more of the nice-to-have items, until the profit stood at 30% of the deal. This would mean Mauritz and John would recoup their capital inputs. It also meant we could walk away from the scrap metal missions. This contract would be our ticket to stay in Iraq.

We celebrated in advance that night, and the next day went fishing. Rieme had befriended a guy in the Green Zone who knew of a small inlet next to the 14th July Bridge where Saddam Hussein and his friends had apparently gone fishing. Only potential problem was that the inlet was a little exposed and you had to sit low down the embankment in case a sniper decided to take pot shots.

I have to admit that this fishing expedition was bizarre. Here we were in the middle of a war zone, standing at the water's edge, fishing. It did not seem right.

We only had one rod so took it in turns. Mauritz cast first and soon landed a strange-looking fish, which was probably Nile perch, or a similar species. I was next and had the same good fortune. But what we were after were the monster-sized carp we could see being attracted by our bait, which was nothing more than bread. Rieme's friend hooked one and played it for a while before bringing in what must have been a 10-kg carp. As he was releasing it the military police arrived and told us to move out as there had been hostile activity across the river. It was a reminder that even when you were having fun, violence and death were never far away.

Back at the hotel I decided to dispense with my staircase run and swim instead, convincing Eddie and Mauritz to join me. I told them that when I'd checked the previous day the water had reached a swimmable temperature. But that was no longer the case. It was now so cold I thought my head would explode, and it took all my willpower not to gasp from the shock. I swam a length and could hear Eddie bellowing with surprise at the cold. I turned for the second length but I was starting to freeze and could only do two more lengths.

By the time I climbed out, all the waiters were standing around looking highly amused. After I'd downed three coffees I checked the pool's temperature. It was back to eight degrees. Apparently the warmer water had been drained the previous day and the pool had been refilled with clean water for the

FIRST MAJOR CONTRACT

summer season. The joke was on me. I should have checked before diving in. I don't think Mauritz or Eddie ever forgave me. And that was the last time we used the pool.

We had ten days to wait for word on the Al Muthenna air base contract. We had done as much of the sourcing of material as we could and that was as far as we could go. It was maddening and frustrating but we had to sit on our hands and wait. Nevertheless, we kept to our daily routines.

During this time we attended the meetings of the Private Security Association of Iraq. There were indications that rules and regulations were tightening up. The licence agreements for private security companies were in the final draft phase and were expected to be passed in the near future. These would require that companies had to register with the Iraqi Ministry of Trade and acquired the necessary licences.

One of these regarded weapon permits. The Ministry of Interior was worried about the number of guns in the country and the increase in gun trafficking. Already all companies who worked on US Department of Defense contracts had to have letters of authorisation indicating which staff were entitled to carry weapons. These authorisation letters were signed on the completion of a shooting competency test, which, in turn, had to be signed off by the contracting officer. Everyone carrying a weapon also had to sign the rules regulating the use-of-force code. And a copy of all this needed to be kept in each man's file.

In March 2004 cellphones arrived in Iraq. There was instant demand and we learnt that a Greek had control of the sale of SIM and recharge cards in Baghdad. His prices were high: $100 a SIM card and $25 for the recharge cards. But if we wanted connectivity immediately we had to pay or wait months. I arranged to meet him at his office to buy the cards.

The Greek's shop was a nightmare of crowds hustling noisily for SIM cards. No one took kindly to me pushing through but I managed to get to the manager in his small office up a flight of stairs and down a narrow corridor. He had the pay-as-you-go SIM cards that we needed but not the contract SIMs. These we would have to get at the Babylon Hotel.

'Don't tell anyone I sold you these,' he said to me. 'There will be a riot in my shop.'

Getting the contract SIMs was much easier as there were no queues at the hotel. I didn't understand why this was the case and asked Hassan about it. He explained that only the rich could afford contracts. I had brought an old spare phone with me and gave it to Hassan until we were able to buy him a new one. He was over the moon. As all the cards were in Arabic, he first had to show us how to recharge airtime and check our balance.

Before I could call home, I first had to figure out the international dialling code, which I found online. There was quite a delay on the line, but it was amazing to be able to speak to Vivienne and the kids.

Once the ten days were up, Mauritz, Eddie and I met with Rick. The contract was signed, he said, he was just waiting for the financial approval, which was a mere formality. I told him about our situation with the temporary passes to get into the Green Zone and asked if he could give us a letter which we could use to get DoD or embassy badges. Our free lunches would be a

FIRST MAJOR CONTRACT

thing of the past if we did not get the DoD badge, since it gave you access to the embassy and the DFAC.

Rick said he would see what he could do and that we should come back after lunch. Before we ate, we walked around the PX to see whether any new stuff had arrived. Mauritz nearly bought everything in the shop. We were still enjoying our lunch when Rick joined us. In his hand was an A4 envelope containing the clearance letters for our embassy badges. 'You'll also get DoD badges once the contract is signed,' he said.

I immediately phoned Rieme and Snoeks and told them to come to the embassy to get their badges. It seemed I had just put down the phone when they walked in. We didn't waste any time going to the badging office with our letters, and minutes later we all stood there with our flashy yellow embassy badges. I wanted to show everyone my badge, I felt like Superman. After months of struggling to get around town and around the embassy, in a mere 20 minutes that had all changed.

After that, we went back to the hotel to wait for Rick's call that the finance had been cleared.

Having cellphones made all this so easy. (Interestingly, the US Department of State had their own cellphone network, and although they could phone us we couldn't phone them. We would later be issued with two embassy cellphones. The calls on these lines were free, which meant phoning home carried no cost. To our dismay John took one of these phones.)

Given that the financial clearance would not take long, John was advised to return to Iraq and we started planning the recruitment of personnel. This would be handled by Gerhard Nel, the CEO of Safenet Security in South Africa, and I would fly home to select the 40 guys. They would need to be equipped and issued with uniforms. Time was tight, but I had already contacted my network of men in the Gauteng region. There were more down in Pietermaritzburg. Those selected would have four days to wrap up their affairs before flying out to Iraq.

This was all going to mean an immediate outlay of finances on equipment and air tickets, but as the contract would be paid in full upfront and in cash we would have the money to cover the expenses. Mauritz later told me that they'd collected the money from a vault under the US embassy that was chock-full of cash. Billions of dollars stacked on pallets.

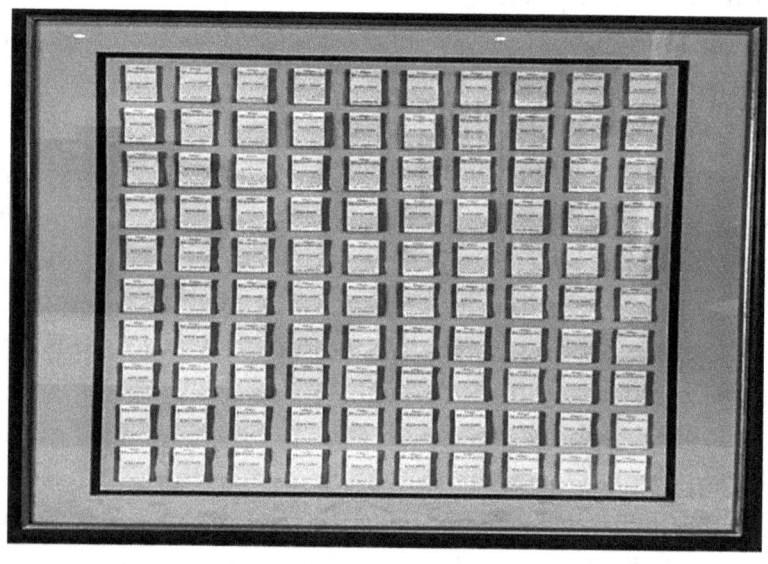

OSSI/Safenet co-owner Mauritz le Roux had the binding from the 10 000 stacks of dollar bills framed

A marine had counted out their three million from one of the pallets and they'd carried it away in two suitcases, one and a half million dollars in each. For his part Mauritz didn't want to take his eyes off the suitcases, and spent a very uneasy time gulping down his supper in the hotel dining room that night before rushing back to the suite to ensure the money was safe. We soon started referring to this payout as 'Monopoly money'. Talk about throwing money at a problem.

In the days before John arrived, we spent the time checking out the Baghdad International Airport so that we could clear our new staffers through it quickly. We left early one morning and, thanks to the embassy badges, made it through even the toughest checkpoints. Hassan knew his way around the terminal buildings and we soon had the lay of the land: where the drop-off points were; the parking areas; what sort of searches were conducted (a dog search at the entrance to the terminal buildings); and discovered that with embassy badges we could accompany our clients and take our weapons inside.

Our task completed, we had brunch in the nearby Camp Victory, a US military base that had the biggest military supply store and fast food places (including a Burger King) in Iraq. The coffee and the burgers were something else. Pleased with our morning's work, we bought a burger for Mauritz and headed back to the hotel.

On the airport road – Route Irish – we were some way behind one of the high-profile PSD teams. As they took the off-ramp to the Green Zone, I noticed three insurgents leap out from under a bridge and run into the road. One had an RPG-7 and the others opened fire with AK-47s.

The RPG-7 is a particularly impressive rocker launcher. When it is fired it emits a huge flame at the back but there is no recoil to speak of. The projectile is a shaped charge with a copper cone inside. The copper cone melts as it penetrates the armour plating, splattering copper drops that burn and cause injuries to anyone in the target vehicle. A direct hit on an armoured vehicle will destroy the vehicle. Just the noise of the explosion will ensure that any passengers left alive are confused and stunned.

From my days in the Border War I had fired and been fired on by RPGs. However, bush war is one thing, urban warfare is another.

Seeing someone running around a highway with an RPG was unreal, it was out of my context for war. I realised then that there was no way we could ever identify the enemy. The only way of telling foe from friend was when weapons were produced.

At first we didn't know if we were the insurgents' target or the PSD teams ahead of us. But when the insurgents turned their backs on us I knew we were in the clear, and radioed Rieme to warn him of what was going down not 200 metres ahead.

When the RPG was fired, the rocket hit the target's back window in a huge flash of fire and smoke and skewed the armoured vehicle across the middle of the road. By now we were almost on the insurgents and roared past them into the smoke and dust. My worry was that we'd get caught in the crossfire between the PSD team and the insurgents behind us.

Normal practice was for PSD teams to support one another. But we were in soft-skin vehicles and they were our disguise and cover. If we stopped we would be vulnerable and would alert the insurgents to our mode of operation. There had been times, and would be times, when we would stop to help teams in trouble but these occasions always depended on the circumstances and what sort of mission we were running at the time.

Right then, we needed to get off the highway.

I alerted our PKM gunner to be ready for any attack from the rear. We were about to take an off-ramp and I didn't want a repeat of the situation we'd just witnessed.

FIRST MAJOR CONTRACT

The notoriously dangerous Route Irish, close to the entrance to Baghdad International Airport.

It wasn't the first time we'd seen a contact and it wouldn't be the last time. No matter how bush-hardened we were, no matter our training and combat experience, there was always a spike of adrenaline, you were always nervous and afraid.

In that moment, when the adrenaline rushes in, everything seems to slow down and your ability to evaluate and discard information is amazing. Decisions are made in an instant, and this is where training and experience help you to stay calm under fire and to function as a team.

This attack brought home the reality of Baghdad. Undoubtedly Route Irish was the worst road in Iraq. Insurgents knew they were hitting high-profile targets and, as there was only one road to the airport, ambushes and IEDs were a daily hazard. It was a road no one wanted to travel. But it was a road we had to travel often.

Just the next day we were to collect John from the airport and would have to drive along Route Irish. It was a prospect none of us relished, so it was a tense team that set out for the airport. We spoke very little on the way there, our eyes searching ahead for any sign of trouble. Fortunately we were able to collect him and get back to the hotel without incident. It was a relief to step into the Al Hamra.

But then we had nothing to do but wait for the call from Rick. By late afternoon everybody was on edge and we decided to head for the embassy. I remember sitting in the dining room drinking coffee after coffee while John and Mauritz were in Rick's office. They seemed to be away for too long and I began to imagine that something was wrong. Then, there they were striding towards us with big smiles on their faces. It was all systems go. In fact, we were expected to be up and running in 14 days.

Mauritz undertook to contact Gerhard in South Africa to get the equipment together while John would alert his office in the US to start preparing for the payroll details and the banking transfers.

My problem was booking a flight to South Africa. Flights to Dubai were booked out for the next few days but I could get a ticket to Amman the following afternoon. Now that Royal Jordanian Airlines was flying into Baghdad it was relatively easy to get a connection to Amman. Our days of missions to the border post were seemingly over.

I was going to have to buy tickets for each leg as I went along.

This was tricky. There was a flight from Amman to Dubai a few hours after I landed, but if I missed it I would have to take the morning flight. On the Dubai to South Africa leg there was only one flight a day and it left at five in the morning. I could end

FIRST MAJOR CONTRACT

up spending a lot of time in transit. It didn't bear thinking about.

The next morning, Eddie and I attended the intelligence meeting. The route to the airport had been declared black by the embassy. This meant that only mission-critical Department of Defense operations would be permitted on the road.

As we knew, a team had been hit the previous day, but what we didn't know was that three PSD guys had been killed. Also military personnel had been killed in a separate incident when a car bomb was driven into their convoy and exploded.

This ratcheting up of the tensions in the city was the last thing I wanted to hear.

After the meeting we collected our DoD badges, which meant we were now a fully qualified PSD company. Once we'd replaced the MP5s with AK-47s I'd be happy.

In the early afternoon I left for the airport along the notorious route now classified black. I'd decided that it was too risky for the team to make the run. Instead, we went in Hassan's old Chevrolet Dolphin, which sported an automatic gearbox with only three gears. It was rusted and had a hole in the bonnet. You could not get a vehicle more low-profile. Taking only my laptop bag and a rucksack, and wearing a shemagh, the two of us headed for the airport. I couldn't take my weapon or body armour because Hassan would not be able to drive around town with it without the correct badges.

Since we were going low-profile, we had the windows open to look like the other locals on the road. Route Irish was quiet that day with only civilian vehicles on the road. I didn't want to compromise our low-profile cover and told Hassan I would only use my DoD badge in an emergency. At the checkpoints we queued with the other vehicles and were waved through. No one realised I was an expat. But at the main airport checkpoint we hit trouble.

The marine sergeant ordered us to get out of the car, convinced that such a rust bucket had to be a car bomb. He made me walk towards him with my hands in the air. I did as I was told, as I did not want to be shot by a panicky 20-year-old.

As I got closer and he could see my DoD badge, he realised I was an expat and told his soldiers to stand down.

'Hell, man,' he said, 'you could've been shot.'

I lowered my hands, explaining why I was travelling in an old civilian car dressed as a local.

'In all the time I've been here, I've never seen this before,' he said, apologising for pointing guns at us. 'You know I can't take any chances. Sir, if you'll just clear your weapon.'

'I'm not carrying a weapon,' I said.

'No? You haven't got a gun?' He couldn't believe me. No one with a badge was going to go around unarmed. He ordered a search of the vehicle to make sure I wasn't lying.

As we drove off I heard him say to one of the marines, 'Another crazy South African. They're all the same.' He tapped his head.

13
The best-laid plans

My flight to South Africa was not without its tense moments. Getting from Baghdad to Amman was no problem, but once there I found that Royal Jordanian Airlines had overbooked their flight to Dubai and there was a crowd of angry passengers causing mayhem at the check-in counter. And here I was without even an onward ticket.

Eventually the airline arranged for the disgruntled passengers to fly on a British Airways flight. Which was fine, but I still didn't have a ticket.

'I can't help you, sir,' said the attendant at the check-in counter. 'You need to buy a ticket first.'

'Please,' I begged. 'I have to get home. My child is seriously ill in hospital. He might even die. This is an emergency. Please can you issue me a ticket.'

The hopelessness on my face convinced her and she booked me through to Dubai. I spent the flight wondering if I'd face the same hassles trying to get a ticket to South Africa. But that part all went without a hitch, and I arrived in South Africa late in the afternoon.

Gerhard met me at the airport and told me on the way to Pretoria that he had already bought everything the guys would need and even packed each guy's kit into a bag. When we went out to dinner we each phoned 15 of the men in Gauteng to arrange interviews for the next day. These went well – there were many familiar faces from my days in the army. Fortunately most of the guys had no problem with the quick four-day deployment. Having spent time in the army, they were used to sudden departures. I selected 22 candidates and put a number onto the relief list as we would need stand-ins when the guys went on leave.

John and Mauritz flew out to South Africa with the cash in their suitcases two days after me. I had to smile thinking of the two of them on a plane with three million dollars. Neither of them would sleep. Every time anyone opened the overhead luggage bins where their suitcases were stowed they'd be as alert as hawks. But that would be their problem.

The following day I drove to Pietermaritzburg to find about 50 men keen to apply. By nine o'clock that evening I had finalised the interviews, which meant I could overnight at home before driving back to Pretoria the following afternoon.

After the months I'd been away, it was wonderful seeing Vivienne and the boys, although the time was far too short. But one night and a morning was better than nothing. We kept the boys out of school so that I could at least spend a few hours with them. I have to admit, though, that between time spent chatting with them I was also emailing personnel information sheets to the US office for processing so that the air tickets could be purchased. Our men would be flying out in groups of 15, the first group being the Pietermaritzburg contingent.

In the afternoon I had to bid my family goodbye and drive back to Pretoria. Saying goodbye was something you never got used to.

For many in that initial batch, this was the first time on a commercial flight. For many, it was the first time out of southern Africa. When we were all together at OR Tambo I briefed them about what they were to expect as they went through the check-in, the security checks and passport control, and gave them the news that this was a 'dry' contract. The wives who were with them had big smiles on their faces.

I also went over the living conditions in Baghdad and at the site so they could be prepared for what lay ahead. I also briefed them on the project and what was expected of them.

'You want a last beer, now's the time to drink it,' I said.

My parting words to Gerhard were that I'd never seen so many lost souls together. The whole business of getting through check-in and the passport and security checks left most of them looking like rabbits caught in the headlights, their eyes wide with bewilderment. And these were battle-hardened soldiers. I had to explain everything to them, from the smokers having to put their lighters in their check-in luggage to all metal having to be removed from their pockets when going through security.

I rounded up my lost souls and we made our way to the departure lounge. Our flight was Joburg to Dubai, Dubai to Amman, Amman to Baghdad.

'The next time you do this,' I said, 'you're on your own. No more Uncle Neil to shepherd you through.'

I have to admit I felt a bit like a schoolteacher explaining the world to a class of nine-year-olds, even down to how the on-board television worked.

The clincher came in mid-flight, when a very pissed-off flight attendant accused one of the guys of smoking in the toilet. I couldn't believe he had been so stupid.

'We're going to lay charges and you'll be arrested when we get to Dubai,' she said, angrily.

This was not the sort of event I wanted. I needed to resolve this, as no one would want to be locked up in Dubai – or any Middle East country for that matter.

I had a quiet word with the flight attendant explaining that he was in my charge and Afrikaans-speaking and didn't understand English very well. I apologised profusely. Said he'd seen the ashtray in the toilet and thought it meant he could smoke. Also that it was the first time he'd ever been on a plane and was unfamiliar with the rules.

'I'm responsible,' I said. 'It's my fault this has happened.'

It took me an hour to convince her not to lay charges. The fact that he'd not denied the allegation worked in his favour.

'Anyone pulls a trick like this again, that person's on the next flight home,' I informed them all.

In Dubai I spent time doing a recce of the airport, as I suspected I was going to be seeing a lot more of it over the coming months and years. From there we flew on to Amman and overnighted in a hotel. There was a small restaurant across the road from the hotel and I decided to give the men their first taste of Arabic food. They loved the fresh bread and all the rest of the meal. I just smiled, because I knew the novelty would soon wear off.

I had to buy a Jordanian SIM card and asked if anybody wanted to come along. Most of the guys joined me. I knew the others were probably going to the hotel's sports bar but I wasn't concerned as I knew the guys would have a heart attack when they saw the prices of the alcohol. A beer cost the equivalent of R100!

I was able to find a cellphone shop and also bought a new phone for Hassan, a Samsung that flipped open. I had seen how he looked at John's similar phone – he would be the envy of Baghdad.

THE BEST-LAID PLANS

The next morning we took the red-eye to Baghdad. Rieme met us at the airport with SUV taxis and the two Nissan Patrols, and the new guys had their first introduction to life in Iraq. They were issued with AKs and magazines, told to wear their body armour, told to take off their sunglasses.

'I catch anyone wearing sunglasses, I'll shoot you myself,' Rieme told them. 'Keep your weapons in your bags and don't load unless I tell you.'

I think this was the first time the men realised they were in a war zone and that there was a high probability they could be killed. Suddenly the laughter ceased. Everyone was quiet and serious. This I expected from old soldiers and knew how they'd be feeling. What had seemed like a fantastic adventure while they were still in South Africa was suddenly a very real conflict situation. Just the trip from the airport to the hotel – what with shot-up buildings and the remains of car bombs – was enough to show the reality of violence-torn Baghdad in 2004.

At the hotel we briefed them about daily routines and meal times, as well as the vital details such as when to use their weapons, the rules of engagement and our evacuation plan in emergencies. No one was to leave the hotel complex unless they wanted to use the internet at the Little Flower across the street.

I was pleased to see the new men settling in quickly and adapting to the tension of their new environment. Back in South Africa I knew the next groups were preparing to depart. Out of the 52 guys I'd hired only two had ever flown overseas before. These two were appointed as leaders for the next groups that would fly in, as they knew what to expect.

As if to emphasise the seriousness of the situation, that night there was a mortar attack on the Green Zone. We heard the explosions and sirens and ran to the rooftop to see what was going on. I estimated about 15 mortars had gone in. On the roof with us were the CNN team broadcasting live to America. At one point they zoomed in on the military supply store and reported that they could see fire and smoke. I had to smile because I knew the smoke was simply from the new generator at the store. It just goes to show you can never believe everything you hear on the news!

Over the preceding months we had become good friends with the reporters from CNN. They were all ambitious journalists, each one hoping to get the next big story that would enhance their career. In our conversations they could never understand that for us this was just another job, something we did to pay the bills. They often asked to do a story on us, but we always declined. Given the South African government's stance on private military contractors, we didn't want the spotlight on us.

In the following days we ran missions collecting the new guys from the airport, at the same time getting them used to driving on the right-hand side of the road and working in convoy, with the lead vehicle calling in any unusual vehicles or pedestrians ahead and the gunship alerting everyone to any suspicious vehicles coming up from behind. A vehicle with more than two occupants was considered suspect as they could be insurgents. We went through the techniques for high- and low-profile missions, especially the need on low-profile missions to use the queues for locals at checkpoints rather than following the other PSD teams through the military lanes. I bought shemaghs for everyone.

It was during these missions that one of the new guys told me about GPS systems and how Google Earth could be loaded into these devices. He showed me how to generate and print a map of the route to the airport for each vehicle. I was impressed, this would surely make our lives much easier. I immediately emailed Gerhard requesting that he sends us six Garmins.

I also took the guys to the airport site so they could see what it looked like, and we also started clearing some of the rubbish from the buildings. In fact, within a day or two we made such good progress that we were able to install the generator and set up a kitchen. I informed Mauritz and Rick that we would be deploying a day early at the site.

Later that morning a Humvee patrol arrived, and I was approached by a sergeant and asked what we thought we were doing.

'We're deploying here tomorrow,' I told him, showing him Rick's letter of authorisation.

'Shit, man,' he responded, 'someone could've told me about it. We're at the base just past the range.'

'Yeah, I know,' I said. 'We were going to come over tomorrow to discuss how we could support each other in an emergency.'

'Listen, pal,' he said. 'Can I take that letter.'

I had a copy so let him take it, but I was worried that word of our deployment hadn't been issued to the relevant people. Something did not seem right.

I phoned Mauritz and told him what had transpired. He tried to get hold of Rick but the phone rang unanswered.

'We better get onto Rick chop-chop tomorrow,' I said. 'It's probably just a slip-up but we need to sort it out.'

I disconnected and we were about to leave the site when the Humvee sergeant arrived with a lieutenant from the Department of Justice. I knew the shit was about to hit the fan. First thing the lieutenant wanted to know was who was the contact for the contract.

'Rick Clay,' I told him.

'That right,' he said. 'Well, I gotta tell you Rick and his boss and some Blackwater guys have been arrested for illegally selling rebar to local engineering companies.'

I smacked palm to head in exasperation. 'You got to be shitting me.'

'Sorry, guy,' he said. 'That's how things stand. You're not to deploy.'

So far: so much money spent, so many arrangements made, so many men recruited.

We went back to the hotel so that I could debrief Mauritz. 'Better tell John to get here quickly!' I said.

A major concern was that we'd spent a fair amount of the contract money and we were committed to paying the guys three months' wages. I had promised these men work, and sending them home with nothing would be disastrous for them and their families. To have 40 men sitting around in the hotel while we tried to find another contract was going to set us back $150 000 a month.

John got onto a lawyer and the matter was taken out of our hands. Many months later the upshot was that we did not have to pay back the money.

14

The battle of Fallujah

With the Department of Defense contract in tatters, Snoeks decided in April 2004 that he would take a leave break in South Africa. As the cheaper route home was to do the first leg overland from Baghdad to the Jordanian border and then to Amman by taxi, he took this option.

We'd become experts in the border run and usually travelled in the dark early hours of the morning, as any night ambushes would be over or abandoned and IEDs were of no concern as the insurgents didn't recognise two vehicles as a PSD team. We left at midnight, wearing body armour and with loaded weapons. This was, after all, the triangle of death we were driving through.

The roads were empty and there was little traffic on the highway. Hassan and I were in the first vehicle; Rieme, Eddie and Snoeks behind. We were travelling at about 140 km/h and everything looked smooth and easy.

Then about 10 km from Fallujah we noticed that vehicles were doing U-turns in front of us. At first we were worried that these might be insurgents planning to backtrack on us and attack from the rear. We thought an attack was imminent.

The next moment I saw in the Nissan Patrol's highlights an Abrams tank in the middle of the highway with its barrel pointing at us. Not a position anyone would wish to be in. Next to the tank stood a marine sergeant with a flashlight, waving us down. We stopped and stuck our DoD badges out the window.

'Road's closed,' said the sergeant. 'You got to go back to Baghdad.'

'We've got badges, why can't we get through?' I asked.

'Road's closed,' he repeated.

'For how long?' I wanted to know.

'Could be a few days.'

'What do you mean, that doesn't make sense.'

Which was when I heard the unmistakeable sound of an airstrike.

'We're attacking Fallujah,' said the marine. 'This is as far as you go.'

American Humvees on the highway to Ramadi and Fallujah.

I could hear Snoeks swearing over the radio.

'Look,' I said to Snoeks, 'we can buy you a ticket on Jupiter Airlines for this afternoon flight. Hassan's got contacts. You'll still make the Dubai connection.'

We got back to the hotel at about two o'clock. I decided to alert the CNN team to the attack, and they soon had news teams on the story.

'How'd you find this out?' their intelligence officer, a middle-aged woman, asked me. She'd been asleep when I came banging on her door.

Over coffee I told her about the tank in the road and the sergeant's information, adding that we could hear the F-16s attacking Fallujah.

This was major news for them, and from then on the CNN crew's attitude towards us changed; it was almost as if we became one of them.

Thanks to Hassan, Snoeks managed to get an air ticket to Amman so he could make his onward flight. But it irritated him that he'd had to go this route.

'Why'd they have to wait until the day I'm flying home to launch a strike?' he kept asking, as if the US had done it deliberately to thwart him.

On CNN they reported that this was a revenge attack for the killing of the Blackwater men.

15
Near misses

The unexpected was a constant in Baghdad's daily life. You could never say a day was normal because every day had the potential for death and disaster. You never knew if it was your last day together. It was always a bit strange returning from a leave break. One moment you were enjoying the comfortable family routine and the next you were in Baghdad, facing the constant threat of death or injury on PSD missions.

The Border War had been much like this, and without that experience operating in Iraq would have been difficult. We were on our own. Often, if something happened to one of us, no one would be any the wiser. Not having communication with other security companies was a problem: if there was an issue we needed to be able to alert someone.

For me, the major concern was medical support and how to repatriate a critically wounded colleague. I needed protocols to handle these issues.

One Friday morning – a quiet day in Muslim countries, with no traffic, as the shops only open in the late afternoon after prayers – we decided to have lunch at the embassy. Eddie also wanted to ascertain from the hospital whether they had various emergency medical items that we needed.

I remember thinking on the way to the embassy that even for a Friday the streets were particularly quiet.

In the embassy dining room we joined a table of fellow South Africans and spent a pleasant few hours catching up on their news and news from home. I'm sure rugby was part of that conversation. Certainly ice cream would have been part of my pudding. As we were leaving, one of Rieme's friends invited us over to their villa that evening. He worked for Olive Security and they had a villa in the Green Zone.

'We're having a little jol, you should come over.'

'Lekker,' I responded. 'Be good to meet other guys. We're getting tired of our own stories. See you later.'

We piled into our vehicles and set off for the hospital. No sooner were our wheels rolling than the embassy sirens started up and the loudspeakers warned of incoming missiles.

Mortars? Rockets? Who knew? And they might be random firings and come down anywhere.

Had we been in an armoured vehicle I wouldn't have felt half as exposed, but right then in the Nissan Patrols we were sitting ducks.

'Not good,' I said to Rieme who was sitting next to me.

'Bloody right, not good,' he replied.

Snoeks and Eddie were in the second vehicle and the next moment I heard Eddie screaming over the radio: 'Go, go, go! Mortars!'

One exploded right behind Snoeks and Eddie, the next exploded beside my vehicle. I felt the blast, and the Patrol shook. Rieme reached out to steady himself with a hand on the dashboard.

I floored the accelerator and made a sharp turn towards the hospital, hoping to get out of the line of fire. The last mortar had been almost on us. We mightn't be so lucky with the next one.

We pulled up some distance later under some trees and waited.

'Five blasts,' Rieme said. 'Close call.'

What had saved us were concrete Jersey barriers down the centre of the road, dividing it into two lanes. They'd absorbed the blast and the shrapnel. If they hadn't been there the vehicles would have been badly damaged and we would most likely have been injured.

'You almost bloody rolled us taking that right turn,' Rieme said as we inspected the bombsites.

'Ja, but look at the line of fire,' I said. 'It's a perfect line. If there'd been another one it would've taken us out.'

'I reckon,' said Rieme.

We were both amazed that the vehicle's windows were still intact. Somewhat rattled, we decided to head back to the Al Hamra. I knew the Green Zone was a magnet, but in the middle of the day, and a Friday at that, this attack just did not seem right. It was a lot safer in the Red Zone.

All the same, that night we were back there for the braai and party at the Olive villa. It was humming with clients and civilians. The food was fantastic – it was a braai after all – and given the day's fun and games we broke our rule and had a beer. Or two.

The party waxed and waned, with people drifting off and returning throughout the night. Mostly the clients were British and Americans and pretty soon they were all hammered. There were other parties in the Green Zone that night and these people rotated between them. Clients in the Green Zone lived life to the hilt.

We had a good time and were well hosted, mostly by youngsters who I thought probably didn't have a clue what life was all about. When you've had a mortar explode beside you, it does shade your thoughts on the meaning of life.

By eleven o'clock we were off, because that's when the

checkpoints closed. No ways was I sleeping in the Patrol that night.

We had another near miss on a mission to Kirkuk a few months later. Kirkuk is in northern Iraq, about four hours – some 300 km – from Baghdad. We'd slept over in the city and left early in the morning. Shortly after the town of Tikrit – about halfway to Baghdad – the traffic came to a halt. US convoys used this route, consequently IEDs were frequently detonated by insurgents.

I suspected an IED had been found, and settled down for a long wait. Sometimes it could be hours before the bomb disposal teams arrived.

We were in our preferred low-profile mode so could hardly force our way through by travelling counterflow, the way a high-profile team would have done.

In these sort of traffic queue situations, the locals get out of their vehicles to find out what's happening, and indulge in a bit of bantering conversation. I asked the local guys with us to climb out and join their compatriots. Eventually word came back to us that there was an unexploded IED up ahead and that the military had erected a checkpoint.

About then I noticed that no one had got out of the three vehicles in front of us. This was immediately strange. If one or two had got out, I wouldn't have thought twice about it, but this set off a red light.

'Hassan,' I said. 'Listen, won't you go see what's going on in the BMW in front of us. Nobody's got out. That's strange, hey?'

'It is,' he said, cracking the driver's door and hopping out. He inserted himself amicably into a group of locals chatting near the BMW. The group gave him good cover to observe the BMW and the GMC in front of it.

Hassan returned, a frown on his brow. 'They're insurgents,' he said.

I got on the radio to our other vehicles and told them the situation. 'Just be ready for a fight,' I said. We were parked in and there was no way we could turn around as the car behind our convoy had blocked the road.

This was not a good situation. Minutes ticked by. Five, ten. We sat there, alert, ready for something bad to go down.

Vehicles crossing the railway line on the gravel bypass road outside Tikrit. The insurgents' car was just ahead of us, making this an extremely dangerous situation.

Then I noticed up ahead that people were getting back into their cars.

'We're on the move,' I radioed to the convoy. 'We're going to stick behind the insurgents.' The last thing I wanted was for them to somehow manage to fall in behind us, as we'd then lose a decided tactical advantage.

We moved slowly off the main road and crossed the railway lines onto a gravel bypass road. This road I knew was in a terrible condition and at times we might be four cars abreast as we negotiated the potholes and gullies. But we had no option. We were acting like locals and had to remain acting like locals. I didn't want anyone realising we were a PSD team.

Over the railway line the road was worse than I'd imagined. The traffic created clouds of dust so that we could see only a few metres ahead. Cars were slipping and sliding about with alarming randomness as drivers fought to avoid the potholes. There was no way we could maintain formation. I went on the radio.

'Guys, just keep moving with the flow,' I said. 'If you have to stop let me know. Otherwise we'll regroup when we're back on the main road.'

By now we were weaving between the BMW and the GMC and I could see that Hassan was right: they were insurgents; I could even see their weapons. One minute we'd be in front of them, the next we'd be behind. And this is how the positioning went for the next 40 minutes. We were way out of my comfort zone.

Fortunately, with all the dust the insurgents were not looking around and had their windows closed. We had fitted film to our windows that made it difficult to see who was in the vehicle.

For those 40 minutes I sat with my weapon on my lap, ready to fire. If one of those insurgents had raised his rifle I would have shot. I was not going to give them the initiative.

When we were back on the tar I asked Hassan to pull over and check the tyres. This would give us a reason for stopping

IN THE KILL ZONE

These items were always on your lap or between your legs during missions so you could react immediately. The satellite phone also had preloaded contact numbers.

and allow the rest of the team to close up. A couple of minutes later we were in convoy and back on the road.

Shortly before the IED site the BMW and the GMC came roaring past us in the opposite direction. They must have panicked at the sight of the US military guys who were directing the traffic.

Once we were back in Baghdad I let out a sigh of relief that we had not ended up in a firefight. It seemed wrong that we'd been so close and just let them go. I was reminded of my army days in the recce wing when we sat and watched and never got involved.

But I had to remind myself we were a security company and not a military unit. We were not there to eliminate the enemy but to ensure that our clients were safe.

Once again, our low-profile approach had served us well. The insurgents had no idea we were there. I was reminded of the words of a warrant officer during a training session at Fort Doppies, a Special Forces base in the Caprivi Strip. He would always say, 'Look through the bush, not at the bush'.

He taught me that things aren't always what they seem.

16
Villa T-Bone

Although we were financially in the black, despite the cancelled contract, keeping 46 guys in the Al Hamra was costing a lot of money. It now made sense to find a villa.

In April 2004 Hassan was tasked with locating a property close to the hotel, as we knew the area and it seemed relatively safe. Within a few days he came back with a prospect a mere three minutes from the hotel. It was a free-standing villa with a three-metre-high perimeter wall.

The house had two storeys, five bedrooms, three bathrooms, a huge dining room and kitchen. There was also an underground basement. The landing on the second floor was ideal as an ops centre. The flat roof could be turned into a gym and braai area. The power and water pressure were good, and there was a pump connected to the mains to keep the water pressure constant.

The villa was owned by an elderly man who wished to join his family in Jordan. He was asking $60 000 for the rent on a 12-month contract.

'Tell him that's way above our budget,' I said to Hassan who was translating. 'Tell him $40 000.'

But this was too little for him, so we haggled and settled on $52 000. He threw in the furniture as an added extra. In other words, it would cost us a little over $4 300 a month. This was a huge saving, given the size of our hotel bill. All we needed was to buy a few more beds.

A couple of days later, the rental contract signed and the

money transferred, we moved 20 men into the villa straight away and got the basics, a house cleaner and guards, up and running. There were air conditioners in three of the rooms but the power was more off than on at that stage. Additional air conditioners and a generator would have to come at a later stage. This meant that some of the guys took strain in the early summer heat, but I knew this was an issue that would soon enough be resolved.

The team that moved in here clubbed money together to buy some gym equipment and added a braai. The basement became a transit camp for new recruits prior to their being dispatched on contracts. The villa was soon named Villa T-Bone, a name that lasted for the six years we lived there, and probably originated at our first braai on the property.

As the company expanded over the coming months we were able to employ support staff, and eventually Gerhard was brought in to take over my job. I was asked to start the most lucrative project the company would acquire.

During March and April that year we were extremely busy, and matters were changing on a daily basis. In fact, things almost ran out of control. We'd landed a contract with Environmental Chemical Corp (ECC), and without support staff we were running security, booking flights for those going on holiday and new staff, recruiting, and buying vehicles, weapons and ammunition.

We were importing armoured GMC vehicles from Mexico and Brazil; these were older-model GMCs that looked like the common local taxis. Once we'd fitted them with red number plates, no one would know the difference. We'd ordered them specifically to meet the requirements of our low-profile missions. However, getting them cleared through customs was a nightmare. Also on order were three sedans.

Vehicle repairs were now becoming an issue, and eventually we brought in our own mechanics. Our 'soft skin' vehicles were being upgraded with protection plates. On top of this, there was staff induction training, and taking care of clients was proving demanding and almost a full-time occupation. We were also tendering on contracts, which meant research and the compilation of proposals.

In addition, I was playing referee to keep Mauritz and John from killing one another. There was no trust between them. Yet even in this chaotic and hectic time the company flourished, mainly due to the quality of the guys on the ground and the brilliant work that Snoeks and Rieme did on the projects. These were the best sorts of advertisement for the company.

Our contact with ECC had started at the function arranged by Rubar Sandi at the end of the tour by American contractors being chaperoned by Stephanie Jasen. Mauritz had met the CEO of ECC, Rick Ebil, and, as they were based in the Flower Land Hotel across the street, he maintained contact, introducing Rick to John.

One day John went over to the Flower Land to smoke a cigar with Rick. This was his method of doing 'business development', as a client's caution would usually be down in such an informal situation and they might share valuable information. Once again, it worked. Rick had told John that ECC were likely to win the Kirkuk Military Training Base (KMTB) project in Kirkuk, valued at $120 million.

At the time their security provider was a French company, and although he did not want to loose them, he doubted they had the capacity to handle the project. Rick wanted the security team to be on the ground a few days after the contract was awarded to impress his client, the Air Force Center for Engineering and Environment (AFCEE). If ECC could have their team ready in time, it stood a good chance of winning other AFCEE contracts.

John, ever the old CIA operative, analysed the problem and came up with a solution. In short, this meant absorbing the French into our company. As we already had personnel in the country, we could deploy 30 men immediately to Kirkuk.

'They're all ex-military,' John emphasised. He had always been a staunch supporter of South African Defence Force members. 'They've all seen action in the Border War in Angola. You could not get a better team with more actual experience. What's more, the team leader is an ex-Special Forces operator with years of bush war experience.'

It didn't take more than a few puffs on his cigar for Rick to buy the plan.

When John broke this news to Mauritz, their relationship became even more hostile. Mauritz had believed that Rick was his client and saw this as an attempt to sabotage that relationship. John and Mauritz were fiercely competitive, and this would eventually lead to the break-up of the company. As I was the man in the middle, and as both men loved to micromanage, this emotional see-saw would wear me down too.

Right now we faced the very real possibility of landing the ECC security contract; John just had to get the French to buy into the plan. As managing the finances was a full-time job, it was decided that Snoeks would select a team and get things under way in Kirkuk. He was the ideal person: a brilliant planner who paid close attention to the smallest detail. It would be up to him and the project manager to work out how the base would be protected and to establish a villa complex for the protection team. One drawback was the single route to the site, which meant they could be targeted by IEDs. Low-profile missions would not work here, as the team would be driving the same route every day.

Snoeks Niewhoud (left) with one of our clients at a villa in Kirkuk.

Meanwhile John, who could speak French, had talks with the French owner/operator, Jean Philip. They came to an arrangement that kept the French unit as an entity within the OSSI/Safenet family. There were benefits for them, as they now fell under our insurance policy, and we scored by getting access to their armoured vehicles.

ECC won the contract and Snoeks was deployed to Kirkuk after selecting his team. Luckily we still had all the equipment from the cancelled contract; we only needed to buy the vehicles Snoeks would need.

VILLA T-BONE

Initially, the operations centre was located in a room at the Flower Land Hotel. We kept this in place until the Villa T-Bone was operational, and then relocated. Here we could plan and dispatch missions more effectively and we found that mixing the teams – French and South African – worked well. Fortunately everyone clicked. The French even took to low-profile missions.

Very quickly, an operational routine was established and we felt we were running a tight efficient security business. ECC appointed a new security manager, Alfred (Al) Habelman, a former US marine who made up for his lack of in-country experience by being highly professional, with a sharp eye for the best interests of the client. He was known to be exacting when it came to missions: always checking routes and alternatives and insistent on a final inspection before a PSD team was deployed. Yet he and I were soon to have an altercation.

I recall on one sunny Baghdad morning when a bomb exploded near the Al Hamra, where I was still staying at the time. In fact, the blast blew out windows of the Al Hamra and the Flower Land, and I was knocked out of my chair by the pool. My first reaction was to rush to the gate, anticipating a ground attack. Fortunately I seldom went anywhere without a concealed pistol, so at least I had some firepower. Of primary importance was to ensure that the checkpoint was in position and unharmed and able to repel any forces that might attack the hotel.

It turned out that the guards had not been injured, as the bomb had targeted the Australian embassy further down the road. I placed everyone in good firing positions, as I expected a secondary attack. This was almost standard procedure with terrorists – to follow the first bomb with a second or to initiate a ground attack.

We stood there waiting, tense with anticipation. I heard someone running and turned to see Alfred Habelman sprinting towards me, followed by a PSD team leader.

'We're going to look at the bombsite,' he said.

'No, you're not,' I replied. 'No one is leaving the hotel grounds.'

'I'm a marine,' he shouted. 'I know how to handle myself.'

'I don't care who you are. I'm being paid to look after your safety and there's no ways you're going out of this gate until the military has cleared the scene. There could be a secondary attack at any moment.'

He got very angry, but I wouldn't budge.

'Calm down,' I said. 'You can help me with security at the gate. This is our prime concern until the threat is over.'

By now CNN's security, armed to the teeth, had joined us. They told us the power had gone down in the hotel.

'Okay,' I said to Alfred, 'I'm going back to phone the ops room to cancel all in and out missions until we have clearance. You're in charge of the gate.'

The next day Alfred apologised to me for his attitude and said I was right to stand my ground.

'Actually, I'm impressed with the whole team's reactions,' he said. 'Their first concern was the clients. They're real good professional operators.'

Crisis moments like these definitely helped to cement our relationship with ECC.

That bomb blast spurred ECC into finding a villa, which turned out to be only 150 metres from Villa T-Bone. They felt, with the hotel being so close to the embassy and near two other hotels, it might be a regular target.

Eventually they would hire the whole block and we were

able to establish a safe compound. Neil van der Merwe, the man I had saved from arrest for smoking in the aircraft toilet, would become the compound security manager.

17
Ordinary deaths and cloak-and-dagger work

Amid the turmoil of writing proposals for contracts, organising the logistics of men and equipment, and just keeping up with the day-to-day running of the company, we had not paid any attention to drawing up standard operating procedures. If someone was killed in a firefight we had procedures in place, but what if someone died of natural causes? I hadn't even considered this possibility. Until it happened.

One of the ECC contracts was to build schools. Part of the schools project was to give the kids sports such as football. One of the construction engineers on the project, Shaun Fyfe, had coached Little League football and had been a professional football player himself until an injury to his knee put him out of the game. He was a man well liked both by his colleagues and the kids.

One Friday in June 2004 he approached Eddie for painkillers, but our protocols were such that Eddie could not assist clients with non-emergency medication or treatment. For these complaints they had to see the doctors at the military hospital in the Green Zone. Al Habelman duly made arrangements to take Shaun to the hospital the next day. Saturday mornings were usually quiet times for us, but a phone call to let me know that Shaun was holding up the PSD team was to darken the day.

Al and I went up to Shaun's room, and when he didn't respond to our knocking and calling I fetched a spare key from reception.

The moment I opened the door I knew something was

drastically wrong. You could smell death, and this meant that he had been dead for a while.

Shaun was lying on the bed, half dressed, clearly dead.

My first fears were that he'd been murdered by terrorists, but there were no wounds, no blood, no signs of a struggle and he'd not been strangled. He had the sheets pulled back and clutched in his hands. It looked to me as if he'd been in a lot of pain before he died.

'Don't touch anything,' said Al. 'This is now a crime scene. We'll have to tell the US police and FBI. I don't suspect foul play either but we've got to let the embassy know.'

I stayed in the room while he alerted the authorities.

Shaun's death was confirmed as natural causes and his body taken to the mortuary in the Green Zone prior to being flown back to the US.

This incident made me realise that the last thing we wanted was one of our guys dying of natural causes and his body being taken away by the Iraqi police. I was convinced it would never be seen again. It was time to pay closer attention to our standard operating procedures so that they were in place to meet all contingencies.

With the addition of the schools project to the ECC contracts I now realised that we desperately needed another armoured vehicle. The older-model GMCs John had ordered were still on the high seas from South America. I put out the word through Hassan that we were in the market for an armoured car. They seldom came up for sale, but in Iraq anything was possible.

Eventually I was approached.

'There is a problem,' I was told. 'This vehicle is owned by

one of Saddam's generals. He is wanted by the Americans but now he is a senior officer in the Mahdi Army [the militia of a hard-line Shiite cleric called Muqtada al-Sadr that spearheaded the first major armed confrontation against the US-led forces from the Shia community] in Sadr City.'

Sadr City was about 10 kilometres outside central Baghdad. The asking price was $25 000.

'You can look at it,' said my go-between. 'It is in very good condition. Blue Mercedes-Benz that even belonged to Saddam Hussein. Made for him in the factory.'

The story was that if I wanted the vehicle I would be taken to Sadr City by one of the general's bodyguards. No one could follow or they would be shot at the Mahdi Army checkpoints.

'Do you trust the general?' I asked.

'Of course,' came back the quick response. 'Very honourable man. Since Saddam's time I have worked with him.'

This didn't allay my fears, as I could see my life ending up in an orange jumpsuit prior to a beheading.

That night I discussed the deal with Rieme and Eddie. We had the money for the vehicle, but that wasn't the issue. The issue was being at the mercy of Mahdi soldiers. The Americans would have a tough time getting me out, even if they knew where I was.

'I'll go,' Rieme volunteered. 'I look more like a local.'

I shook my head. 'Not going to work.'

'Then maybe don't take all the money,' Rieme suggested.

'Ja, that crossed my mind, but then what if the vehicle's right and everything's good. I don't want to do this twice. Anyhow, not having all the money might piss them off.'

I've been in some tight spots before but this felt like it was pushing the envelope.

'I'll have my phone,' I sighed, resigned to the inevitable. 'At least I can phone if things go wrong.'

A meeting was set up and I drew the money. I took a bag to the meeting but the money was stuffed into my underpants. If they snatched my bag, I would still have a bargaining chip. I took two phones, so that if the one in the bag was taken there was a back-up in my sock. Sure, I'd have to take my boot off to retrieve it but this was better than being left without a phone.

I was nervous waiting to be collected. It felt like I was back in the bush war. Except now I had no weapon and I had to rely on the bad guys to look after me. This was playing Russian roulette with two rounds in the chambers.

My lift arrived and the man spoke perfect English.

'Do you have a gun?' he asked.

'No.'

'Do you have a tracking device?'

No again.

'I believe you,' he said. 'I am not going to check. But if the general finds you are lying it will not go well with you.'

'No worries,' I said.

We left the hotel and went in a direction that was not towards Sadr City.

'Where are we going?' I asked. 'This is not the right way.'

He laughed. 'So you know Baghdad.'

'I've been driving around it for the last few months,' I replied.

'We are taking a back road to make sure no one is following.'

This, too, caused me concern as it meant that they were going to great lengths to ensure no one knew where we were.

Under an overpass we stopped and changed vehicles, and this time headed for Sadr City.

Entering Sadr City was like entering another country. The atmosphere was tense and people dressed differently, in more traditional clothes. At the Mahdi Army checkpoint we were waved through. At the next checkpoint I was blindfolded.

'It is not far now to the general's house,' I was told.

The blindfold was reassuring, as they would not have bothered if they had no intention of releasing me.

About ten minutes later we stopped and the blindfold was removed.

The general stepped forward to greet me.

'You are not an American,' he said. 'Where do you come from?'

I told him.

'I like South Africans,' he said. 'They have done a good job in Iraq.'

We then had tea, and afterwards I was taken to examine the vehicle. It was spotlessly clean and looked brand new although an old model. I could see it fitting perfectly into our operation. You only knew it was armoured when you opened a door. The window glass, too, was armour-plated. The engine number and the Vehicle Identification Number (VIN) were original. The fan belts were new and the battery terminals clean – always a sign that a vehicle is well looked after. The engine started on the turn and purred like a cat. I could not have been happier.

Now all I needed was to get out alive.

Custom dictated that tea be served again. While we partook the general told me that he had used the vehicle to get home after Saddam's palace was attacked. He'd kept the vehicle at his house but did not want the Americans to find it or he would be in trouble. I didn't tell him he was in trouble anyhow.

Then the haggling started. This was expected but it was the

ORDINARY DEATHS AND CLOAK-AND-DAGGER WORK

last thing I wanted. I wanted to pay the money and get the hell out of Dodge.

I opened by citing the market value of $20 000.

'This one is in such good condition, people will pay more. There are lots of people who will pay more.'

We both knew this was not true, as the market for armoured vehicles was hardly large.

'All right,' I said. 'I will pay $25 000.'

Which was where we settled. When I undid my pants to take out the money he burst into laughter.

To his aides he said, 'This is a careful man who does not put all his eggs in one basket.' He laughed some more, enjoying his own joke.

I gave him the money and he handed it to his aides. Immediately they started counting it, but he stopped them.

'Where are your manners?' he asked. 'This man will not cheat me.' Then he turned to me. 'I apologise, my friend, but you will be blindfolded again. This is for your safety. We will drive the vehicle to the checkpoint and then you can take it. You will be escorted out of Sadr City. You know the streets of Baghdad, my people tell me.'

We shook hands.

'I hope you get many happy miles,' he said. 'You will be safe inside because everyone knows it was mine.'

I had to drive back to the hotel with the fuel light on red. All I needed was to run out of fuel and get stuck on the side of the road. However, I was also sure I was being followed, and this was actually reassuring as I knew there would be no issues.

To say that I was relieved when I drove through the hotel gates would be an understatement. The guys were soon swarming over the vehicle in admiration.

'Where the hell did you get that from?' asked Al Habelman. I told him.

He stared at me in disbelief. 'How did you get there and back?'

'Long story,' I said, and proceeded to tell it.

It would not be the last time I'd buy cars in Sadr City, but of all my buying forays there, it was the most cloak-and-dagger operation.

18
Expansion and new contracts

As the extent and value of our contracts increased, it became increasingly urgent that we acquire another villa. ECC had hired five villas in a block not 150 metres from Villa T-Bone, and, with the permission of the few private householders, we were able to secure the whole area with round-the-clock guards and a sentry point with a boom gate. T-walls and towers were erected and all the PSD vehicles were now parked within a secure yard.

The villa complex had numerous routes in and out, which meant the PSD teams could alternate their routines, making it difficult for any possible surveillance by insurgents to gain accurate information. For the Al Hamra Hotel it was a sad day in July 2005 when we all finally moved out, because we were the last of their anchor tenants, CNN having moved out a few months earlier.

One of our new clients was a medium-sized American construction company called Tetra Tech. I am not sure exactly how we secured the contract but it might have been that on a flight from Dubai to Baghdad, John had met Dale Carruth, Tetra Tech's CEO. They were both military men and soon got together regularly to chat over whisky and cigars. This friendship led to our running the odd PSD mission for Tetra Tech.

Then Tetra Tech landed the substantial Camp Rustamiyah contract to build a huge base complex for the Iraqi army, including a water treatment plant. (Camp Rustamiyah was the site of the oldest army academy in Iraq and was used as a US military forward operating base for a while.) The site was way out of town on the highway to Kut, an alternative route to Basra in southern Iraq. We were asked to bid for the security contract.

In November 2004 I took a team to recce the site, which turned out to be in a truly hostile area. The adjacent US military base, Camp Cuervo, was attacked almost on a daily basis. Insurgents would launch mortars from across the river, knowing that any retaliatory force would have to ford the river before they could attack. The moment the Americans did this, the insurgents would disappear.

At the time, the site of Camp Rustamiyah consisted of some bombed-out buildings and two bunkers. These bunkers I reckoned could be used as accommodation for the security team, and we would be able to defend them with armoured vehicles and mounted machine guns. The site was huge and was going to take some planning in the entry and exit points and the storage area of building materials, at least in the initial stages.

The plan was to use Hesco defensive barriers, which had proved their efficacy in the first Gulf War in 1990–1991. Dale was under the impression that these could be erected in a week but I estimated that a double stack would take at least two weeks to complete. Once the 250-page security plan was compiled, I met with the colonel in command of Camp Cuervo. He was in charge of the security of both camps in this hostile region and asked me to come directly to him if I had any security concerns. This was a useful channel, as normally I would have gone through the project manager.

The project was due to start in five weeks and we were to present the security plan in the preceding week. The initial billing for the project was $1,4 million. There would be two PSD

The bunker that we called home for several weeks on the Camp Rustamiyah project.

teams and 22 expat personnel and 160 locals on the project. As the project progressed the guard force would be decreased. The end-plan billing would be about $650 000 a month.

As Gerhard was to join us (with a group of new recruits) and as I was ahead of the game, I decided to take three weeks' leave back home.

I flew to Durban where Viv and the boys, who were 17 at the time, collected me for the drive up to our home at Mtunzini. It was good to sit in my own home on my own furniture, enjoying a bottle of wine with my wife, my sons asleep in their rooms. Right then, Mtunzini felt like a long way from Baghdad.

But the next morning I realised it wasn't. I was up early, before the rest of the family, checking my emails in the kitchen. The first email I opened was from the contracting officer, apologising for getting the dates mixed up. We did not have four weeks until the security presentation; it was scheduled for two days' time and we would have to deploy five days after the presentation. I immediately emailed Gerhard about the change in plan and asked him to do the presentation.

This was the last thing I had expected. It had been a long time since I had been home and I had so looked forward to the time with the family. I had planned fishing trips to Richards Bay and surfing with the boys, and I wanted to spend time with Vivienne. To say I was pissed off would be putting it mildly.

Still, this was what we had been working for all this time. It could put us on the map in Iraq. To drop the ball now would have been a bad move. So, I would be flying back to Dubai on the evening flight to help get things ready for the deployment. I was going to take the team in for the initial start-up.

I had to wake my long-suffering wife and ask her to take me back to the airport. I have to say that Vivienne took it very well, even if the boys were upset that our deep-sea fishing expedition wasn't going to happen.

By the time I got back to Villa T-Bone, Gerhard had made the presentation and we had five days to get everything ready. The plan was that once the protective walls and the towers were erected, the client's engineers would be allowed on site. At first we would need a small force to protect the people constructing the wall, but this would be increased as the project progressed.

For the use of our security equipment, we invoiced the client on a monthly basis. As most projects ran at least a year behind schedule, our profit margins on the equipment were healthy and a single project was often sufficient to pay off the cost. This meant that when the equipment was moved to the next site, the rental we received would be pure profit.

EXPANSION AND NEW CONTRACTS

On schedule we deployed our staff and three of the six Mambas – armoured personnel carriers – that we'd acquired. We were six expats, four Angolans from 32 Battalion and ten Iraqis. On our way to the site there was an unfortunate incident.

On an off-ramp on the Dora Expressway, Bret – our PKM gunner – noticed a vehicle travelling towards us faster than most of the traffic. One insurgent tactic was to ram into a target vehicle and then detonate a bomb. He radioed me: 'Guy coming in, could be trying to break our security.' We were on an open channel, so everyone in the convoy could hear the conversation.

In incidents such as this we had clear rules of engagement issued by the Americans. These had to be followed before deadly force could be used. Bret now went through the procedure.

First he warned the driver using hand signals and commanding him to stop. All this came through to us as a running commentary.

Next he showed his weapon, a clear display that we were about to fire live ammunition.

Still the driver paid no heed.

Our fear at this point was that the vehicle was a car bomb, technically known as a **VBIED** (vehicle-borne improvised explosive device), and that they intended to crash into our convoy and trigger a bomb. The explosion would kill most of the people in the armoured vehicle if the bomb was big enough – often a combination of artillery shells, TNT and some other explosive. The easiest places to break the security of a convoy were on an off-ramp or at an intersection. Which was why we were on full alert as this vehicle roared towards us.

In a last effort, Bret hurled a water bottle, but the vehicle did not slow down or turn away.

I ordered Bret to open fire.

He did, firing six rounds at the vehicle. His target was the car's engine but some shots were a little higher and killed the driver.

I then notified our ops room, who in turn contacted the US Military Operations Centre, who issued a warning to others to stay away from the location.

All PSD teams were tracked by the military at all times. The Operations Centre looked a bit like a cinema with a large screen showing the position of all the PSD teams they were monitoring as well as their own teams (they had about 20 operational).

From the moment the vehicle had been spotted to the moment we engaged with live ammunition, about 20 seconds had elapsed. In some cases, when the threat was imminent, the action would be even faster.

The military did not like incidents in which we were forced to take action. They were bad for the US image and the image of the security companies. We didn't like them either, as they were a threat to our lives.

After such incidents, our policy was not to stop as the car bomb could still be triggered, and once a convoy was stationary it was open to attack. It was regrettable that people might have been killed or injured in the incident, but stopping to give assistance might have resulted in many more deaths.

This attack was not a good omen for the start of the project.

As mentioned, our intention was to live in the bunkers at Camp Rustamiyah while the project got under way. Unfortunately shepherds had used the bunkers at night to keep their sheep safe

EXPANSION AND NEW CONTRACTS

and they were ankle-deep in manure. Cleaning them was not going to be a pleasant job, but much to our relief the shepherds came asking for work and we put them to cleaning the bunker.

We positioned the Mambas defensively and posted guards, and I sent Hassan to look for food. In those first days we did not have a generator to run a fridge so would have to live off whatever local food supply we could find. This was clearly not going to be a problem, as Hassan returned a mere 20 minutes later with ten roasted chickens and chips and 30 samoon breads.

'There's a place close by,' he said. 'We can get breakfast, lunch and supper.'

Roughing it was not going to be all bad. We had food, and we had a stove so we could make coffee. I could put up with most things as long as there was coffee.

I had expected the subcontractors to arrive at noon, and on the hour they did with two excavators, a bulldozer and five flatbed trucks loaded with Hesco barriers. These are blocks of reinforced steel mesh that were stacked and then filled with sand. The first stage of the perimeter wall was to protect the bunkers. This would shield us from attack, and any insurgents would not be able to see us walking around.

With the turret of the Mamba just high enough to see over the Hesco wall, we were in an excellent defensive position. At night we could reverse the Mambas into the bunkers and they would seal us inside. The only passage would be through the turret. Each of the vehicles would have two expats on duty for shifts of two hours each.

But while our security was tight, portable toilets – one for the expats, one for the locals – had not been delivered and would only arrive the next day. Nor were there any showers yet.

The guys on that team were a happy-go-lucky bunch, quick

to laugh, and nothing seemed to get them down – not even the freezing cold of the long nights. The wind snaked into the bunker and we were unable to warm ourselves no matter how warmly we dressed. Each morning, Hassan's first job was to collect firewood so that we had heat while we boiled water for coffee. He then went off to buy our breakfast of roast chicken, chips and bread. The bread was hot and delicious. I couldn't always face chicken three times a day, so I varied my breakfasts with a samoon cut in half like a bun and filled with cheese and honey. Now that was a first-class breakfast, washed down with coffee.

The perimeter wall of the Life Support Area (LSA) at Camp Rustamiyah, with the bunkers in the background.

That second day, we made a makeshift door, complete with frame, so that the bunker could be closed at night. On top of the bunker a guard post was constructed with a double layer of sandbags and a roof.

EXPANSION AND NEW CONTRACTS

That night, we dined on chicken and rice. I hoped it would not be too long before the client was on site with a proper kitchen. We'd look like chickens if they continued as a major meal.

For washing purposes, I asked Hassan to buy large plastic basins. He looked at me as if I was mad, but I had used this system many times in the bush, having learnt the technique from the Bushmen, and it would do here.

That night I took the biggest pot we had and added six litres of water. This I warmed on the stove. The guys stood around wondering what I was doing. When the water was warm enough, I poured it into a plastic basin, undressed and sat in the tub. I then washed using the lovely Lifebuoy soap we'd brought from home.

Everyone stood around in stitches of laughter, telling me, no way would they be washing like this. But by bedtime they'd all been through the process. For many, this procedure was a first. There was photographic evidence of this event but the pictures have gone missing. Possibly deliberately.

The next morning we had a visit from the contracting officer. I gave him the grand tour – with coffee – of the bunker/barracks/office, the guard post, the perimeter fence (which was only partly filled with sand although no terrorist would ever realise that) and our security plan, including the guard duty shifts.

'You guys ever want a shower,' he said, after I'd explained our bathing arrangements, 'I can organise it across the way in Camp Cuervo.'

There was some enthusiasm for this option.

'We want to get started on the project,' he emphasised.

'Once the Hescos are completely filled and we have installed the gates, the security will be tight,' I told him. 'But before that it's too dangerous.'

He nodded his acceptance.

Already the client had appointed a team to clean the other bunker for the engineers to move into. The bunkers were ideal security, especially if rockets or mortars were fired at the site.

Soon we were bringing in personnel from South Africa, putting them through a physiological evaluation and training them. We had guard towers erected, and watched with some consternation the attacks on the adjacent Camp Cuervo site. In those early days on the project, Camp Cuervo was attacked with mortars and there was also a VBIED blast at the main gate. No one was injured but it increased the tension.

On one occasion we witnessed an American patrol ambushed by insurgents from the roofs of nearby buildings. We had to stand by uselessly as the terrorists were out of range of our AK-47s. Had we had a Dragunov sniper rifle we could have engaged them.

However, during the time we were on the site the insurgent activity declined. I was convinced this was because we were hiring locals and they did not want to be killed by accident or lose their jobs. As an added precaution, I insisted that locals had to hand in their phones at the gate – phones were often used to detonate bombs. I was taking no chances. It paid off. For the years that the site took to complete it was never subjected to attack.

When John acquired the Tetra Tech contract he was introduced to another construction company called International Technical Solutions, Inc (ITSI). It wasn't long before they took us on as their clients.

Camp Rustamiyah team members. In rear: Mohammed, Bret Pretzer, Aldo Medves, Jackal (deceased). In front: Jacques Woensdrecht, Sakkie Maree, Marius Crowther, Michael (deceased).

Former members of 32 Battalion who were also appointed on the Camp Rustamiyah project.

ITSI were our first clients housed in the Green Zone. Some of our other clients – such as Tetra Tech which moved there after a car bomb at the gate of their complex was detonated, killing two of our guards – would eventually move to the Green Zone. Or, like ECC, they'd acquire a villa there, although they did not move their entire operation into that sector. Mostly they moved to the Green Zone because their military clients found it difficult to get clearance to leave the Green Zone and this adversely effected ECC operations.

As our relationship with ITSI evolved over the years, we would eventually get our own villa in the Green Zone and ITSI would become an important contract for us. When we moved our business to Afghanistan in 2012 they became our biggest client, and most of the team that supported ITSI in Iraq moved with them to Afghanistan.

The project manager on the ITSI account wanted a PSD team at the villa during the night, although they were in the Green Zone. This worked for us as we could also use that team when the client wanted to move around. However, it was not all plain sailing.

One of the biggest issues we had with the Green Zone was getting the local PSD guards in at the entrance gate at the 14th July Bridge in the morning. Even the correct badges were often not sufficient. Every day we would have to send an expat to facilitate their passage through this checkpoint, a process that even with a chaperone would take time. Although we hated this necessity, we couldn't complain. There was always the project manager to brighten our mood, especially as he was a braai master, and the weekly braai became an event that the clients looked forward to.

Some people think PSD work is glamorous and exciting.

For a number of missions this might have been true, but often missions were nothing more than a glorified taxi service. The team would have to drive the client to a secure location at some military place and then have to sit for hours, waiting for the client's task to be done.

We had two medium-sized contracts with ITSI (one in the south and one in the north), and some smaller contracts in and around Baghdad.

The southern project was remote and there was no US presence in the area. We would take engineers out weekly, and these missions involved visiting police stations where ITSI had construction and engineering contracts. The problem was that local construction contractors used militias for protection because they were cheaper rather than engaging the services of licensed security companies.

We were highly suspicious of these militias, as they were often appointed by the traditional leaders in the area and had no military training and no idea of what was expected of them. Consequently we never felt safe from IEDs, as the checking at the sites was random and casual, nor from attacks by insurgents. We had no idea of where these militias' loyalties lay, and given their lack of discipline there was always the possibility that they would fire by accident and injure one of our clients.

On top of that there was no vetting of the local workforce nor were they searched when they entered the site each day. Security was lax, to say the least. The best we could do was ensure that none of the labourers had access to their cellphones while on site. This eliminated the possibility of indirect fire being accurately delivered.

These were tense and vulnerable missions.

19
In the kill zone

I need to go back a few months as many things were happening simultaneously. At the same time as the airport contract, another avenue that opened for us was the ESS Support Services Worldwide contract. At the time, their core business was food service and cleaning, mostly to the US military and mining industry in remote and dangerous places.

Shortly after the Blackwater contractors were murdered in Fallujah at the end of March 2004, Mauritz met a guy called Bill (we only knew him by his first name), who was the CEO of ESS, at the Al Hamra Hotel. It was a chance meeting one evening while they were sitting beside the pool.

Bill wanted someone to run a mission to the Al Taqaddum Air Base and Camp Fallujah in the volatile region between Fallajuh and East Ramadi. ESS had the catering contracts for both camps. It turned out that Blackwater had cancelled their contract with ESS after the Fallujah attack on the Blackwater contractors.

The ESS kitchen staff had not been changed since the Blackwater ambush and were threatening to go on strike if they were not relieved. The US military either would not or could not assist but had laid down an ultimatum: either change the staff or lose the contract. So, Bill was in the market for a security company prepared to run the Fallujah missions.

Mauritz did not hesitate. 'We'll do it for you,' he said.

'Fantastic,' Bill replied. 'You do those two missions and the contract for ESS security is yours.'

Of course Mauritz was happy at the possibility of another contract, but Rieme and I were less enthusiastic. We were relaxing in our suite drinking coffee when he broke the news.

'You know where those two places are?' I asked him. 'Al Taqaddum and Camp Fallujah?'

Mauritz shrugged. 'Not a clue.'

'They're both in the Sunni triangle of death,' I said. 'The chances of getting the team wiped out are pretty high. Even the military won't go in there.'

'I promised the guy,' said Mauritz.

I looked at Rieme, he looked at me. This would not be easy.

'Thanks for this,' I said to Mauritz. 'We're going to have to get volunteers for this one. It's too dangerous to force guys to run a mission to those places.'

Mauritz said nothing.

I kept on at him. 'If we get the contract we'll have to push the expat pay to $15 000 a month.' I reckoned this would have been in line with what Blackwater charged. It was double the normal pay rates on other contracts but then it was double the risk.

Mauritz didn't quibble. At least he knew how I felt if the contract materialised.

The main route through Fallujah was impossible, we'd have to find another way in. I looked at Google Earth and saw there was an alternative road next to the river that you could access over a bridge close to the city. We would need to recce it.

But, before that, we were due at a meeting with ESS at their villa. Our first mission would be to transport 15 workers to the Fallujah site and return with the 15 who had to be relieved. They were holed up in their hotel and it was costing ESS a fortune.

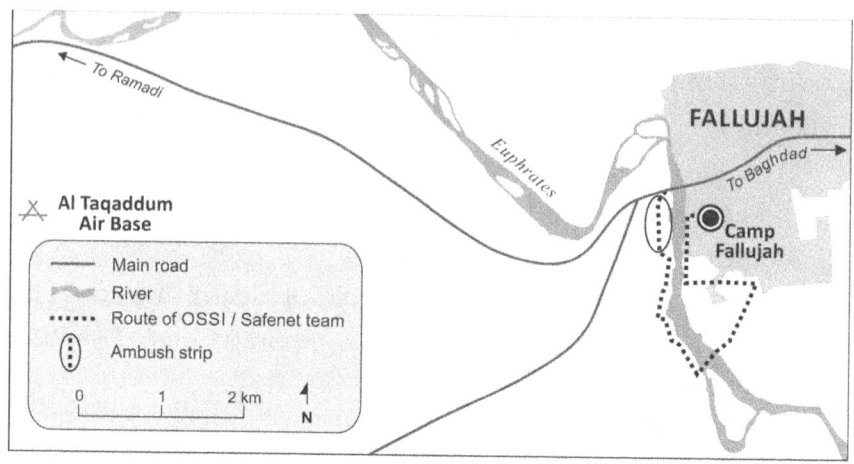

A map of Fallujah and surrounds, showing our route to Camp Fallujah and where we were ambushed.

'That site's difficult, Bill,' I told him over coffee. 'We'll need to do a recce first. I don't want to get your guys killed or injured. Also we'll need you to clear it with the military and tell them we'll be working low-profile as that's the best option.'

'I know what you're saying,' he acknowledged. 'I understand the low-profile idea.'

'Because of the danger, it's going to cost you, Bill,' Mauritz emphasised. 'We're doing this because we hope to sign a contract with you.'

Bill nodded. No one was kidding anyone here.

Back at the hotel we discussed the recce.

'We need one of you with us,' Hassan said. 'Someone to mark the route with the GPS.'

The 'us' was Hassan and our new local guy, Hickman (we struggled to pronounce his Iraqi name, so Rieme had named him Hickman).

'I'll go with you,' Rieme volunteered.

He looked local and the three of them wouldn't be seen as targets. There was always a possibility that there would be an insurgent checkpoint on the river road, and there was no way I would pass as an Iraqi.

The three of them wore traditional *dishdasha*s (long, usually brown or green tunics) to look like the local farmers. (In 2004 these tunics were still commonly worn by Iraqi men. The traditional dress only started to change in about 2008 when Iraqis took to wearing Western-style clothes, even in the deep rural areas.) Rieme hid an AK-47 under his tunic. It was specially tailored with Velcro strips to keep it closed. If he needed to get the gun out in a hurry, all he had to do was rip open the Velcro.

The ideal choice of vehicle was the Kia Bongo truck, as it wouldn't draw attention. Farmers and shop owners used these trucks all the time to transport supplies and produce.

I was certain that if anyone could pull off this recce, it was Rieme.

Which he did. He found the road narrow where there was only one Iraqi army checkpoint at the main highway bridge. Here they were not even stopped. The route skirted the city and entered the base by a back road. This greatly decreased the chances of an ambush; the insurgents would not be expecting us as it was mostly farmers who used this route to town.

Rieme suggested we buy two Daewoo minibuses to transport the clients as these were the most common minibuses and he'd seen them on the back road. My intention was to get them fitted with armour plating, and we'd carry extra diesel drums on the Bongo to refuel the minibuses. I told the ESS people we would need two days to prepare and would execute the mission on the Friday. Traditionally Fridays were quiet with little traffic. It would be about an hour's drive.

The metal panelling meant that the minibuses sat a little lower on their shocks but otherwise you couldn't see that they'd been up-armoured. If we were attacked by men wielding AK-47s the bullets would not penetrate the plates. As long as our clients were lying on the floor they'd be safe.

The only drawback was that the minibuses were slow, with a top speed of 90 km/h if you were lucky. There'd be no chance of pulling away should the insurgents give chase. For our assault vehicles we decided to use the Hyundais. There was no time to armour-plate them so we packed body armour over the seats and against the doors for extra protection.

The low-profile look of the taxis was finished off with curtains, stickers and oddments dangling from the rearview mirror and spread out along the front dash. The windscreens already had a film on – to prevent it from shattering if it was hit by a bullet. They looked like your typical Baghdad taxi.

Four men from South Africa who had just joined us volunteered to run the mission. They had no idea of the danger they faced, and this meant they'd be more relaxed and find it easier maintaining a low profile. Two of them would travel with Rieme and the other two in my vehicle plus a local driver. Hassan and Hickman would be in the Bongo with the fuel drums.

Our plan was to leave at five in the morning. Rieme would lead the convoy, followed by the two minibuses, with my vehicle as the gunship. Hassan would be some distance behind us. We loaded up with medical equipment and enough ammunition to fight a small war. The clients were told that the turnaround time at Camp Fallujah would be ten minutes.

The mission was on time departing. At 05:30 I messaged the ops room that the wheels were rolling. Getting to Fallujah was no problem, as the streets of Baghdad were empty.

IN THE KILL ZONE

At the camp, the contracting officer was amazed that we'd come in such a rag-tag collection of vehicles.

'We were expecting an armoured vehicle convoy,' he said.

'That's the point,' I said, 'this way nobody expects us.' It was said with confidence but I had serious misgivings.

While the clients boarded the minibus and were briefed I spoke to Rieme.

'I think we're blown,' I said. 'On the road next to the river there were some locals that pointed at your car and took a good look at mine too. They were right next to the car and we were driving so slowly they must have seen we were expats.'

'Okay,' said Rieme, 'let's change the sequence on the way back. Put the buses in the front, followed by the Bongo. Then you, then me.'

I agreed. Once we were off the river road and on the main highway we could change back to our original sequence.

I briefed our guys. 'Weapons in hand and ready to fire,' I said. 'We're worried the insurgents might try something.'

Getting everyone into the minibuses and loading up the luggage took a little longer than I wanted, and we were out of the camp after 20 minutes.

My thoughts were that if something was to happen it would be on the bridge. We could be pinned down there.

But that section was clear and we turned onto the river road. Up ahead were a number of men standing next to a vehicle.

'Watch those guys,' I radioed to Rieme.

As I was the driver, I had my eyes on the rearview mirror. After we'd passed the loiterers I saw one run to the boot of the vehicle.

Next minute all hell broke loose.

'Contact! Contact rear!' Rieme shouted over the radio.

IN THE KILL ZONE

In the mirror I saw the guy taking an RPG-7 from the car's boot. There were shots fired from Rieme's vehicle and the RPG man went down. But now the other men opened fire.

Only then did I see there were small groups all along the road preparing to shoot at us. We had no option but to drive right past them. Rieme's guys were giving us covering fire from behind, but we were now in the thick of a firefight. The rattle of the AKs, the smacks as the bullets punched into metal, the shattering of glass, the acrid smell of cordite. We were being targeted at point-blank range with bullets zinging through the car.

About halfway along the ambush stretch I realised the radiator must have taken a hit, as the temperature gauge was in the red and there was oil spraying from under the hood.

The gradient was downhill so I switched off the engine and we freewheeled while the temperature gauge dropped. Then I swung the engine again and floored it. And this was how we made it out of the kill zone to the Iraqi army checkpoint at the bridge. Only there were no soldiers at the checkpoint. They'd legged it the moment they heard the shooting.

'The car's fucked,' I said to Rieme over the radio. 'But we've got to get further away or they'll attack again.'

'Go,' said Rieme. 'I'll cover you.'

Using the same technique, I got us to the highway but knew we were not going to get much further. To my relief there was an American patrol parked at the side of the road. I pulled up beside the Humvee, while Rieme drove on to give our convoy some protection.

'What's wrong, pal?' asked the Humvee captain.

'Didn't you hear the shooting?' I asked.

'Sure did. Sounded bad.'

'That was us being shot at,' I said. 'We were ambushed. You go back there you can roll up the enemy if you want to.'

'Not our mission,' he replied. 'Best I can do is leave two vehicles with you until your recovery vehicle arrives.'

I phoned the ops room for a recovery team.

'Burn the vehicle,' said Mauritz.

'No ways,' I told him. 'I bought this thing a week ago. We're going to fix it.'

Typical PSD mission to Camp Fallujah. Note the cracked windscreen.

While we waited, I checked the damage. The radiator had been holed a few times but luckily they were all at the top. The air conditioner had been damaged and this had sprayed out the oil. Both wing mirrors had been shot off and the front windscreen was shattered. Having film on the inside had kept the glass intact. There were a number of bullet holes through the upper parts of the car doors and the boot.

The Yanks stood around marvelling that no one had been hit. But our local guy was in a state of deep shock. He'd not even climbed out of the vehicle. I took his weapon and made sure it was safe. This was the last mission he would ever do.

We'd come so close to the terrorists. I'd looked one in the eyes. I'd seen hate. At that moment I'd thought: at least I know the face of the guy that'll kill me. My body had tensed waiting for the impact of the bullet. His shot hit the doorframe and ricocheted up, and this had saved my life. In those split seconds, the thought crossed my mind to drive into him but this might have caused damage to the vehicle and trapped us. That's the only reason he escaped with his life.

I received a call from Rieme that his vehicle had a number of bullet holes and the only window intact was the front windscreen. Again, thanks to the film. The body armour over the seats had prevented any casualties. He'd caught up with the minibuses and the Bongo. The Bongo had drawn no fire as the terrorists had eyes for our two vehicles only.

I reckon the main reason we got through the ambush was because they weren't expecting us to return as quickly as we did. Had the turnaround been faster we might have escaped altogether.

Mauritz and the recovery team arrived shortly afterwards and on the way back to Baghdad Mauritz made me go through the event again.

'Just bloody lucky that everyone kept their cool,' I told him. 'Otherwise it could have turned ugly very quickly. A good thing Rieme and I were the drivers. If the locals had been driving we'd have been in trouble.'

Mauritz whistled. 'How many insurgents?'

'About 50 spread along the kill zone. But they hadn't got the ambush set up properly yet. If the RPG had taken out one of the vehicles, we'd have been in big trouble. They only knew it was us when it was too late. The quick turnaround, changing the order of the vehicles, that's what's got us through.'

Something that we often discussed in the coming weeks was the US patrol's insistence on not intervening. We'd given them descriptions, right down to the clothes the insurgents were wearing. Had it been a South African patrol they would have had a go at the enemy. However, that would have left our damaged vehicle without protection.

Mauritz debriefed ESS and confirmed that we would still do the Al Taqaddum mission, much to the amazement of our clients.

'You're going to go back?' Bill asked, amazed. 'I don't blame you if you don't.'

'We want to help you out,' Mauritz replied. Also, we wanted the contract.

That incident was the first proper attack OSSI/Safenet had experienced, and it made all our personnel realise that it was dangerous out there. Many people have made Iraq sound more dangerous than it really was. In truth, like the bush war, not many were involved in any action. Strange that the violence magnets were always the same guys, though. Maybe they signed up for the more dangerous missions.

We never used the river road again as it was too easy for insurgents to attack there or to lay down IEDs. Fortunately, the Americans regained control of Fallujah so we were able to travel safely through the city.

Of course we signed a contract with ESS, and with this financial reassurance were able to hire a villa next to theirs.

It was close to the Dora Expressway, which meant it was easy to get PSD teams out of the city. The only discomfort was the space in the villa: it wasn't that big and the guys were living on top of each other.

Freddy Swan, our magic mechanic, repaired my shot-up vehicle in two days, and it saw service until 2010 when Safenet left Iraq and sold it.

Rieme was appointed the manager on this contract, supported by men who had been in 5 Reconnaissance Regiment and 31 Battalion recce wing. One of them, Evre Hoffman, survived Iraq but later died in an ambush back home. This just did not seem right.

20

Two deadly ambushes

If we had a problematic client it was Al Habelman – the man I'd had an altercation with when a bomb exploded outside the Australian embassy. Habelman was security manager at Environmental Chemical Corp (ECC). Being an ex-marine, he was a consummate professional and took his work seriously. This didn't mean he was always right.

Nine times out of ten, Al insisted on being part of the PSD team during missions to new sites, as he liked to evaluate the security risk for himself. Also, I suspected that if there was the likelihood of a fight, he'd want to be in the thick of it. He was not going to sit cowering to one side. He had his military ID so he was authorised to carry an M4 carbine, and he did so on every mission. He was the only client we had who carried a weapon. On top of that, he would travel in either the lead vehicle or the gunship, never in the armoured limo.

Mauritz had explained the danger of Al's behaviour to the ECC management but they shrugged off any responsibility. The man knew the risks. If he wanted to take them, it was on his own head.

This was not a situation we liked but one we had to tolerate; at least he was a trained and experienced soldier. In total he did not go on that many missions, but the team leaders were not thrilled to have him along for the ride. I rotated his presence with the PSD teams as much as possible to prevent any aggro on a mission.

On one mission to Habbaniyah in November 2005, led by

Leon van Rooyen, Al placed himself in the gunship. They left Baghdad during the night and the outward trip went without incident. The clients were dropped on site and the convoy returned to the city. It was as they made their way out of Fallujah through an industrial area that they were ambushed.

This was a well-prepared ambush, involving both an IED and insurgents.

On this occasion ours was a three vehicle convoy with the armoured limo in the middle. The insurgents let the lead vehicle pass and detonated the IED to target the limo. But they mistimed and the limo went through unharmed. As there was some distance between the limo and the gunship bringing up the rear, the blast didn't effect this vehicle either. However, the explosion was the signal to launch the ambush and the convoy now came under small arms and machine gun fire.

In retaliation, the PKM machine gun in the gunship laid down such a barrage of accurate fire on the insurgents' positions that the ambush petered out.

In the chaos of the attack and the noise when the PKM opened fire, nobody noticed that Al had been shot. When the attack started he was sitting on the back seat behind the driver. During the firefight he had leaned across to return fire out of the opposite window when a bullet through the back window hit him. In many respects it was a fluke hit between two armour plates under his arms. He ended up slumped between the driver and the passenger front seats.

Al was in a bad way but still alive and needed a medical facility urgently. The medic in the vehicle began treatment. The nearest hospital was back the way they'd come, but Leon was of no mind to run through the ambush again. The option was the US camp at Abu Ghraib, some 30 kilometres, or at least 15 minutes, away.

There was considerable confusion during those 15 minutes. Messages were being relayed to our ops room as the situation developed. They were on their way to the hospital. Then they radioed that Al had died but they were going on anyhow so that a doctor could confirm his death. I suspected the bullet must have hit some vital organs.

The vehicle in which Al Habelman was fatally wounded.

When the final details were known it was up to Mauritz to inform ECC of Al's death. Everyone was shocked. He was a likeable guy. He seemed invincible. But on those missions no one was invincible and sudden death was always a possibility. Al knew and understood the risks.

The next day we visited the ambush site and took photographs, as we would need to report the incident comprehensively, including statements from our personnel. It was a tense operation, as the insurgents could still have been in the area. Our men were strategically placed while Mauritz did the walkabout and took the photographs. It was clear that the PKM had saved the day. The insurgents had not expected a return of fire, as most PSD teams were in armoured vehicles and could not shoot back. Judging by the cartridges, I estimated there must have been at least ten insurgents in firing positions. I was happy that the team had done everything by the book and not panicked when the IED exploded. Had Leon decided to make the run back to a hospital in Fallujah we could well have had a second Blackwater incident on our hands.

The inspection done, we collected Al's body from the hospital.

We had taken three GMC SUVs for this mission. The coffin would be in its own vehicle draped in an American flag we'd managed to acquire – a detail that the client appreciated.

The following Friday, ECC held a funeral in the garden of the villa they used as an office. It was a moment when we could all reflect on how suddenly lives could be snatched away, and how suddenly in this dangerous country our reality could change. I thought back to how Al had once argued with me, then had the moral fibre to apologise when he realised he had overstepped the mark. He was a man who lived to the full. And on that warm afternoon under a hazy sky we gathered to pay our respects.

It was a fitting tribute to a well-liked man. A marine who had died in battle. A marine who had died for his country.

TWO DEADLY AMBUSHES

As I've written, there was no normal in Iraq. Normal could include days like this: we were in a four-vehicle convoy for ESS to Latifiyah, south of Baghdad. The convoy was made up of two GMC SUVs, the armoured Mercedes for the senior clients – engineers – with the rest of the clients in a minibus with one of our men.

In the gunship was a colleague from my bush war days, Piet Haasbroek.

About five kilometres outside Latifiyah it became clear that insurgents in two vehicles had decided that the Mercedes and one of the GMCs constituted a PSD team. They went into attack mode, fortunately not realising that the minibus or Piet's GMC – well behind the two cars – were part of the convoy as well.

It appeared that the insurgents' plan was to jam our two vehicles between theirs so that they had a clear field of fire. They did this, and the moment they opened fire on the lead vehicle and the limo, the day went to hell in a handbasket.

Quick reactions and skilful driving enabled the front vehicles to swerve around the insurgents and accelerate away down a side road, but now the minibus and the gunship GMC came into contact with the rebel militia.

Initially, Piet didn't realise that the front vehicles had turned off, and maintained his direction straight towards the town. With bullets zinging and banging all around them, he soon understood that town was the last place he needed to be. They would be trapped in the narrow streets and – three guys against what could become every insurgent in the town – would not stand a chance.

Piet tried to make contact with the minibus behind him, but the noise of the shooting meant his efforts went unanswered. He then tried the ops room on the satellite phone, but also to no avail. By then they were in town and had come to a stop in the traffic. All the side roads were blocked, such was the volume of cars in the gridlock.

To make matters worse, the driver of his vehicle switched off the ignition and fled for his life.

Desperate, Piet decided to run back to the minibus and tell them to follow him as he tried to force his way through the traffic. He had no doubts that the situation would escalate as the insurgents had chased them into the town.

As he made his way between the cars, one of the shop owners opened fire and shot him. Piet spun round, saw the man about to fire again, and with his gun at hip height shot his assailant. The man went down without a whimper.

Piet knew he'd taken a bullet, could feel the pain in his leg, but he was still able to move and reckoned there was no bone damage and, if he was lucky, no arteries had been severed or nicked.

When he reached the minibus he found that the driver had also fled. He instructed one of the clients to take over as driver, dished out two more magazines of ammunition to our man in the minibus, who'd by now exhausted his supply of bullets.

Piet ran the gauntlet back to the GMC and began to force his way through the traffic. It didn't take long for drivers to realise they stood to be rammed aside if they didn't move of their own volition. Such was his focus on the front that when he glanced in the rearview mirror, to his alarm he saw that the minibus had stalled and was about 300 metres back.

He swore, but held his position until the minibus caught up. Together they headed out of town along a road they knew where the police usually manned a checkpoint. By then the insurgents had given up the fight and disappeared into the

TWO DEADLY AMBUSHES

Robert Lundie by the minibus in which our clients were transported.

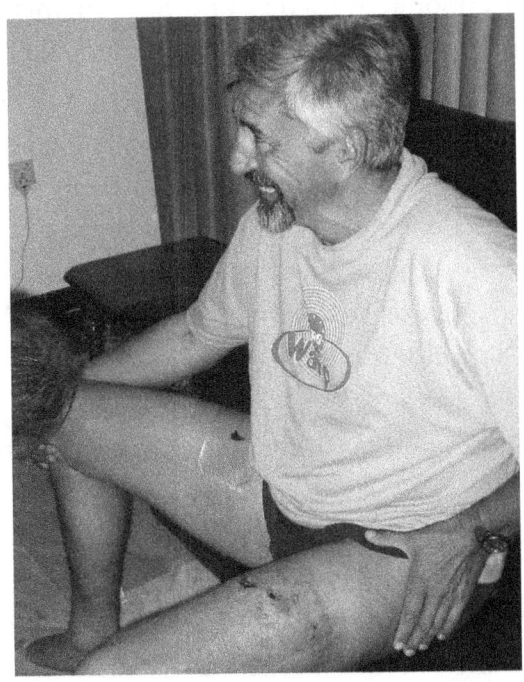

*Piet Haasbroek was hit in both legs by AK-47 bullets.
Luckily, they were only flesh wounds.*

warren of side streets. At the checkpoint Piet confirmed that all our clients in the minibus were unharmed and tried to raise the other two vehicles, but without success.

His bullet wound was painful and bleeding so he decided the best option was to head for the nearest US base to get medical attention.

It had been a close call. Piet survived, our clients survived, and the clients in the Mercedes were not even shot at.

In setting up OSSI/Safenet we'd managed to comply with almost all the bureaucratic checks and balances. We had the necessary US badges, we'd registered the company where we had to, we'd appointed lawyers and accountants, we had the licence from the Ministry of Trade. We were, however, missing the security licence issued by the Ministry of Interior. And now the Private Security Company Association of Iraq was putting pressure on me to fall in line if we wanted to continue doing business in Iraq. The security licence had become compulsory.

I got the lawyer and Hassan onto the matter, but, as Iraqi business practice was not time-driven, neither Mauritz nor I had great expectations that this would produce results any time soon.

'We need to find another way of getting the licence,' Mauritz stressed.

But what other way?

By February 2005 there were more than 30 registered security companies operating in Iraq. Most of these were either American or British. The American security firms were usually tied into American government contracts, which was logical. As we were not trying to compete with them I thought it

TWO DEADLY AMBUSHES

worthwhile paying a visit to Laurence Peters, chairman of the security association.

Laurence was an approachable and knowledgeable guy. He'd assisted in setting up the security regulations and was always available to share his know-how and advice. I set up a meeting at his office in the embassy.

He listened to my story, leaned back in his chair and said, 'Don't go the route using local lawyers. Others have tried it and none of them have been successful. I don't know why. I guess the Iraqi lawyers don't understand the bond process.'

The bond meant that you needed backing in the form of a financial undertaking from a bank as part of the licence procedure.

'You want to get this done quickly, there's a young American lawyer who knows the ropes,' said Laurence. 'He's expensive but he comes through.'

Later that day I phoned the young American lawyer, to be told that the cost was $15 000 upfront. In addition, we'd need a bank bond for $25 000 (which he could help us acquire) and the process would take about six weeks. I arranged to meet him the next day.

Although Mauritz was inclined to give our local lawyers two weeks to get the process under way, I decided that there was nothing to be lost in following Laurence's advice.

The young American was impressive. He ran through the checklist of all the documents we would need to submit. These ranged from VINs, to the types of weapons and ammunition we had, to tax clearances, insurances, social security payments, rental agreements. If those were all up to date, which they were, he'd need a 50% down payment.

'That'll take two weeks to get wire transfers through,' I said.

We stood and shook hands. 'When the money lands, I'll begin the process,' he assured me.

Two weeks later, our local lawyers had got nowhere. In fact, they had not even got an appointment to see either the minister or his deputy at the Ministry of Interior. I went round to the American with all the paperwork and the money. We needed to get the process under way before we lost everything we'd worked for. The only document outstanding was a letter from John and Mauritz giving the agent the legal power to act on our behalf. It turned out that one signature against the Safenet side of the company was sufficient, and I hurried back to Mauritz to get this done.

The agent estimated that the bond payment would take three weeks, and registration a further two weeks. We were within the grace period, but only just.

Five weeks later we were licensed in the name of Safenet. John was unhappy that OSSI had not been included in the company name but I explained that it would have caused a delay that could have been the ruin of the whole company. At least we could continue as normal.

With the expansion of ECC, ESS and Tetra Tech we found that accommodation had once more become an issue, and we went hunting for another villa. This time we had specifications: it had to be large enough to accommodate a complete operations centre, and to be our headquarters, including a store and an emergency room. Preferably it should be in the same area as the current villa because the neighbourhood was safe and we'd be in close proximity to all our clients.

Some months earlier, John and I had looked at a villa that

TWO DEADLY AMBUSHES

Our second villa, which we dubbed 'the Palace'.

One of the bedrooms in the Palace.

at the time was too big, was in need of renovations, and carried an exorbitant annual rental of $250 000. But, as our situation had changed dramatically, it now offered possibilities.

I went back with Hassan and found the place spotless. The renovations had been completed, the air conditioner worked, the garden had been developed. The only (minor) drawback was the dirty indoor pool water, but this was because the housekeeper did not know how the pump worked or what chemicals to use.

The house was ideal. The front door led into a reception room, then to a dining room with a fireplace and a connecting kitchen. The ground floor bedroom was en suite and big enough to accommodate at least 12 people with space to spare. All the rooms were large, almost the size of army barracks. Upstairs were three en suite bedrooms, once again big enough to sleep 12 men per room. The basement was divided into five large rooms with small narrow windows. There was also an outside flat complete with kitchenette, bedroom and bathroom.

From the roof of the main house there was a commanding view over the area. I could see that defensive positions could be built on the roof that would make the villa immune to any type of physical attack. The property also had a garage large enough for six vehicles. The driveway was long and wide and provided parking space for another four vehicles. Outside the gate was a guardroom with a bathroom, currently the housekeeper's accommodation.

The next morning, I gave John and Mauritz a guided tour. They both liked style, and this house had style. It was also a practical option. I explained how we would set up our operation, how the rooms would be allocated and ended up on the roof showing them where the PKM machine gun could be mounted to repel any attackers. Because we were a long way from the road, any car bombs would not make an impact, so there was no need to erect perimeter T-walls. We could keep the villa with its low-profile appearance. Even the roof defences would not be obvious.

One of the aspects I found particularly attractive was the possibility of locating the generator and fuel tanks outside the front wall. This meant that fuel tankers would not need access to the property to refuel our tanks.

John and Mauritz decided on the spot to take the villa, and we moved in the next day, roughing it until all the furniture was acquired. I moved one team out of Villa T-Bone, and the team leader – who loved to cook – agreed to take on the cooking as soon as we'd got pots, pans, cutlery and crockery. Until then we'd be on takeaway rations.

There was considerable chaos to begin with: mattresses were strewn across the bedroom floors, the men were living out of their kitbags, the internet was being installed, furniture acquired, and a safe installed in a small room on the first floor that I intended to occupy. This room also had a window that overlooked the neighbouring property behind us. From here I could cover the rear of the property while the PSD team monitored the front.

What we didn't know was that the palm plantation next to the villa was occasionally used by insurgents to launch indirect attacks at night on the Green Zone. Once the insurgents saw us mounting defensive positions with sandbags on the roof they were not happy. In the first week there was a lot of small arms fire around the villa, which was disconcerting. Fortunately, no one was injured. Still, it was annoying to be

Team members who lived at Villa T-Bone and the Palace, 2005–2006.

woken in the middle of the night with someone taking random pot shots at us. Eventually the insurgents realised we were not moving and took their war elsewhere. None of them was foolish enough to mount a serious attack on us. Our position was impregnable. We named this villa the Palace.

In the coming months and years OSSI/Safenet would hire three more villas around the Palace.

21
Making a plan in Dubai

Part 1

With the PSD teams now in comfortable accommodation and a comprehensive operations centre overseeing the missions, Rieme and I went home for a holiday. Those breaks were always welcome, always too short.

On this occasion we met up at OR Tambo for the flight back to Baghdad via Dubai and were enjoying a last beer when Mauritz called.

'I need you to collect some money from me in Dubai,' he said, sounding irritated that he had to ask this of us. 'We've run out of cash and I have to pay the locals.'

'No can do,' I responded. 'We haven't got visas.'

'Come on, Neil,' he said. 'Make a plan when you get here, even if you have to delay your flight to Baghdad by a day. I'm counting on you.'

Mauritz had bought an apartment in an upmarket building in Jumeirah, Dubai, and was living there when he wasn't in Baghdad. For him the place was home and he couldn't see why we'd have a problem.

Partly he'd moved there because our banking arrangements had been transferred to Dubai, as it was easy to access money there, both in terms of receiving it and paying it out, particularly as we paid our expat guys in dollars. For these reasons Dubai made sense. It also made sense because Dubai had no restrictions on the amount of cash you could take out of the country. In America you couldn't move more than $10 000 in cash, which was never enough for our purposes. South Africa, I need hardly add, does not rate when it comes to international banking. Transferring money was simply too difficult. It was much easier for clients to pay into a Dubai bank account than anywhere else in the world.

Now I thumbed off the connection to Mauritz and recounted the request – no, the order – to Rieme.

'What's the guy think he's doing?' he said. 'We don't have frigging visas. How're we supposed to get out of the airport? Mauritz can seriously piss me off sometimes.'

We said a whole lot more in a lot more colourful language, but that's the gist of it.

'We're just going to have to see what we can do when we get there,' I said resigning myself to a difficult task. 'If we can't get out, we can't get out.'

I had about $2 000 in hand and hoped this would be enough to buy our visas.

This was only my second or third trip through Dubai airport and Terminal One seemed massive. We had checked our luggage through to Baghdad so at least we weren't lugging suitcases around. If we couldn't find a way to leave the airport, we'd simply continue the onward leg of our journey.

We found our way to a visa office.

'We're here for a day and want to check out the city,' I told the clerk.

He told me he'd need copies of our tickets and passports and then an application would be put through to the Ministry of the Interior. The earliest it would be approved would be 10 o'clock the next morning.

'Is there any other way?' I asked.

MAKING A PLAN IN DUBAI

'No chance,' he said, 'you have to have a visa.'

I paid the $100 for the application. We left with no great expectations.

'Maybe there is another way out,' I said to Rieme. 'Worthwhile doing a recce.'

We decided to split up and meet back at the visa office in an hour.

I found a shop selling electronic goods where I hoped to buy a SIM card so that I could contact Mauritz.

No deal. Sim cards could only be bought from the service provider in the city. If I wanted to make a phone call I'd find public phones upstairs, the sales guy told me. I suspected he was Filipino, and I had this idea that Filipinos helped one another all the time and seemed to know a great deal about how the world worked. If anyone knew a way out of the airport it would probably be this sales guy.

'Try the Marhaba service counter,' he suggested. 'They can get you an exit visa because the hotels sponsor the visa. Only problem is you have to take the hotel they give you. At this time probably only the expensive hotels will be available.'

The attendant at the Marhaba desk told me the hotel would cost $250 and the visa $50. 'Keep me two places,' I said. 'I'll be right back.'

When I found Rieme his only comment was, 'Let's do it.'

We paid up, got the visas and headed for the passport control exit. But here we encountered a problem.

'The computer says you have visas pending,' the official told us.

This was true enough. 'When you cancel those it will be all right.'

So we returned to the visa application centre and had our

applications cancelled (without giving the reason) and the deposit refunded.

Passport control now let us through without a problem. I called Mauritz from a public phone and asked him to meet us at the hotel in the centre of Dubai.

'You see,' he said. 'I told you you'd make a plan. When you get to your rooms, phone me again.'

We took a taxi to the hotel, which had to be the grandest place I'd ever stayed in. I'd certainly never seen anything like it in South Africa. Only the hotels on the Dubai beachfront were better than this.

I phoned Mauritz.

'The Radisson, hey! That's impressive. Must cost a lot.' That was Mauritz, always concerned about the finances.

In 2005 Dubai was still in the making and nothing like the place it is today. There was only one shopping mall, and although the airport had two terminals – Terminal 1 for international flight, and Terminal 2 for flights from Iraq, Pakistan and India – this terminal was devoid of shops. You couldn't even buy coffee there.

Mauritz arrived and gave us the money.

'You guys had better check out,' he said. 'We'll have lunch and afterwards I'll drop you at Terminal 2. It'll be time for your flight by then.'

That was my stay in the Radisson. All I got out of it was a shower.

Interestingly, we used this method of getting into Dubai for many years, certainly up to 2012. As long as you had a layover in Dubai airport of at least 12 hours you could get a hotel-sponsored visa. When we were operating in Afghanistan, one way of getting a visa for that country was at the Afghanistan

MAKING A PLAN IN DUBAI

Consulate in Dubai. Our guys would use the hotel-sponsored visa, pay for the hotel, head into town and get their documentation in order. As long as you had an onward ticket and were not round-tripping – for example, Kabul-Dubai-Kabul – you were fine. In the cases where visas had to be extended for personnel already in Afghanistan, we would acquire dummy tickets, in other words tickets booked but not paid for. Once we had the visa we'd cancel the dummy ticket. It's likely that this visa system works to this day, as hotels find it a useful way of upping their occupancy rates.

PART 2

Because Mauritz had a place in Dubai, and because Dubai had a banking system that fitted our needs, and because the company was registered there, it became our business hub, and we appointed a manager, Paul Clark, to run the shop. All the flight bookings were now made here rather than through the OSSI office in Miami, and all spare parts for the vehicles were sourced and bought here as it was the only way of ensuring we got genuine parts. Of course, Paul was also responsible for making sure that everyone got visas when they needed to stop off in Dubai.

As I've said, the leave rotation was three months' duty; 28 days' home time. Those 28 days were much anticipated and appreciated. But there were two occasions when the flights home incurred moments of stress that I did not enjoy.

The first occurred on a flight with ten of the guys. Given that we were flying from Iraq to Dubai for an onward connection, timing became critical. Because of all the flights we had to arrange, we were now booking these through Emirates and had opened a corporate account, which came with many benefits, one of them being priority in booking emergency flights.

On this occasion we were flying Jupiter Airlines to Dubai from Baghdad. As we entered Dubai airspace the pilot announced that we had been diverted to Ras al-Khaimah airport, outside Dubai. Although this was an international airport, it did not cater for flights to South Africa.

Shit, I thought, this is going to be a headache.

There were customs and border control points at Ras al-Khaimah but they did not issue temporary or emergency visas.

I had never been to this airport, consequently did not know the layout. As soon as we landed I phoned Paul.

'Listen, mate,' I said, 'we've got a small problem here. The flight was diverted to Ras al-Khaimah so we're going to need a lift from here to Dubai. I'll phone again when I know what's going on.'

In the terminal building the authorities told us that buses had been laid on to take us to Dubai, and that they could process our visas.

'Problem,' I said to the official directing the passengers to the various queues. 'We've got no visas and we've got an onward connection to catch in Dubai for South Africa.'

He shook his head. 'I cannot help you,' he said. 'I cannot issue a visa.'

'So what're we supposed to do?' There was some consternation and irritation in my voice. 'How're we expected to get to Dubai airport. You land us here and then you don't help us.'

'We can help you tomorrow,' the official said. 'But for now you have to wait.'

Like hell, I thought. I phoned Paul. 'We're stuck. Can't get anyone to help us,' I said.

'Sit tight, hang in there,' he responded.

'Yeah, I can't see us going anywhere.'

'I'll see what I can do.'

'Remember our flights at 5 am tomorrow,' I said. Which gave him about ten hours to sort out this problem.

As I disconnected I saw the Jupiter Airlines pilot enter the terminal building. Maybe he could help? I collared him and explained our situation.

'I am very sorry,' he said, 'there has been a fight between Iraq Airways and Jupiter Airlines and Iraq Airways now has an agreement that they can land at Dubai. Only them. We have lost the licence to do this. I am sorry, but this is why we were told to land here.'

'That's your company's problem,' I said. 'We took your flight on the understanding we would land in Dubai. Your company must resolve this issue and get us to Dubai in time to catch our flight to South Africa.'

This produced no tangible resolution to our problem. About three hours later, Paul phoned.

'I think I'm getting somewhere,' he said. 'The fact that you're on an Emirates flight to South Africa is helping sort out this mess.'

More hours ticked by. Ten o'clock came and went. I reckoned that for Paul to get to us and make the trip back to Dubai would take two hours. Given that the Emirates flight would close its boarding gate about an hour before departure, we would need to leave Ras al-Khaimah by one o'clock at the latest. Any time later and there'd be a strong chance we wouldn't make the flight.

My phone rang: Paul. 'I've sorted it,' he said. 'I've got to surrender my passport to immigration and they'll give me a letter allowing me to fetch you guys and check you in at Dubai

International. Once you're cleared through customs they'll give me my passport back.'

I was relieved. It was 11 o'clock. An hour later he arrived in our minivan which, thankfully, was big enough for us all to squeeze in.

Nobody minded the crush. We were all happy that we'd make our onward flight. And we did, with enough time to spare for a meal and a welcome beer.

Jupiter Airlines were forced out of business by Iraqi Airways. They had filled a gap in the market until the Iraqi carrier was able to get back its planes, which had been grounded in Kuwait and Jordan during the war.

Part 3

Another home visit, another tense moment in Dubai airport. Four of us were headed for South Africa. Two of the guys had been on an ECC project in the north and their trip to Baghdad had been delayed while an IED was cleared from the roadside. Normally we'd get the guys back to Baghdad a day before their flights but on this occasion it had not been possible. So, by the time they arrived at Villa T-Bone we were already in critical mode as to whether we'd make the flight.

Mauritz loved this tension and was always testing the limits to see how late he could be and still make a flight. My preference was to be at the airport hours before the flight. I hated the clock-watching rush.

On this occasion we just made it to the airport in time but the rush had been chaotic and stressful.

In those days Baghdad airport was a security nightmare. You arrived at the first checkpoint outside the airport and the vehicle was checked to ensure you weren't carrying a bomb. The next stop was a luggage check that was done by hand. Here your ticket and passport were also verified. Your luggage was scanned. From here you went to the airport terminal.

Outside the terminal, the luggage was inspected by a sniffer dog trained to detect explosives. Inside the terminal, your luggage went through a scanner once more and you walked through a metal detector.

When your flight was called, you queued at the last checkpoint where again everything went through a scanner. At the check-in counter the luggage was scanned once more before being loaded into the plane. All hand luggage went through another scanner after immigration. Before entering the boarding gate you went through a final checkpoint and again the hand luggage was scanned and you walked through a metal detector. By my count, the hand luggage went through five scanning machines inside the terminal building. Surely this was thorough enough to pick up any explosives or ammunition.

Apparently not.

We arrived at Dubai's Terminal 2 and had to be transferred to Terminal 1 to catch the onward flight. This meant another security checkpoint at Terminal 2 before being allowed to board the bus. I knew this was a mere formality done with a small scanner for the hand luggage and a walk-through metal detector.

We all went through the metal detector and were waiting for our luggage to clear the scanner when I noticed the scan operator getting very excited. He called over the customs sergeant and from then on the temperature rose quickly. Armed customs officials surrounded us, with their hands on their guns in readiness.

'Did you all come on the same flight?' the sergeant wanted to know.

I told him we had.

'Was your luggage with you all the time?'

'Of course. In the overhead bins on the plane.'

Mauritz now stepped forward. 'What's all this about? These guys have got a plane to catch.'

'You must wait,' said the sergeant.

Our hand luggage was snatched away from us and again put through the scanner. One bag was then emptied out on a table. I knew this spelt trouble. I just did not know what sort of trouble. Maybe there was a cartridge stuck in the sole of a shoe. This had happened before.

But no. From the bag the sergeant lifted out a red box with an eagle on it. My heart stopped. This was a box of 9 mm ammunition. Not one single round, but a whole frigging box.

'What's that?' asked Mauritz.

I told him. The blood drained from his face.

I turned to our guy. 'How the hell did that land up in your bag?'

'It was in my grab bag,' he said. 'In the internal hidden pocket. I forgot it was there.'

Mauritz approached the sergeant, explained who we were and why the ammo was in the bag. 'It's an accident,' he said.

The sergeant was sceptical. I could see this was going nowhere.

More and more customs guards were arriving. No one could believe that 50 rounds of 9 mm ammunition was in the guy's bag by accident. I could see us spending the next ten years in jail. We'd all be treated as accomplices. As terrorists.

The more guards who arrived, the more heated became the

conversation, and the more useless was Mauritz's explanation. By now our kit had gone through the scanners time and again, and I assumed they were looking for the gun that went with the ammunition.

'You must wait here for my manager,' said the sergeant. 'This is a serious business.'

A few minutes later I noticed an Emirati official approaching in the customary white clothes that the men wear.

'Our luck's changed,' I said to Mauritz.

'Why's that?' he said. The concern had tightened the skin on his face.

'I know this guy,' I said nodding towards the Emirati. 'Once I had to collect a shipment of radios and he helped me.'

The radios had had to be shipped in a sealed container and he and I had packed them and locked and sealed the container. The accompanying paperwork had been a nightmare. More to the point, because I could not get a hotel-sponsored visa from Terminal 2 we'd struck a deal: he would keep my passport, and he'd let me leave the airport so I could book into a hotel for some sleep. The next day, refreshed, I returned to collect my passport and take the Baghdad flight.

Now the sergeant was telling him what they'd discovered.

He called me over. 'Why do you carry this ammunition?' he asked.

I told him the truth. We carried weapons on a daily basis, we'd been in a hurry to make the flight. The box of bullets had been forgotten in the hand luggage. An accident. We were sorry. Despite the five scanners at Baghdad airport, no one had picked it up.

'I understand,' he said. 'You write a report so that I can speak to the people at Baghdad. Show how lazy they are that they don't do a proper job. This endangers people in Dubai.'

'I'll be happy to do that,' I told him. 'But, listen, we've got to go, our plane's in an hour.'

He arranged a bus to take us over to Terminal 1.

'Safe trip,' were his parting words.

I have to admit that I had a beer in Terminal 1 by way of celebration. For someone who does not drink, this says a lot. In fact, I had a second as well.

Part 4

A final story related to Dubai: before Jupiter Airlines and Royal Jordanian commercial flights flew into Baghdad, we were able to hitch rides on the odd Russian cargo plane from and to Dubai. There was no real booking procedure besides emailing them and asking when their next flight departed. They'd confirm that there was space and you'd rush to the airport. The meeting place was in front of the cargo hangar. The flight cost $200.

On the way back, you'd report at the check-in counter at Dubai's Terminal 3 and they'd send a van to collect you. Your passport would be stamped and off you'd go, having parted with another $200.

On one occasion Mauritz and I were flying to Dubai. We reported to the cargo hangar, paid the fee and were escorted to the plane, an Ilyushin Il-76. Normally they used the propeller-driven Antonovs. This was decidedly upscale, with jet engines; the flying time would be half that of the Antonov.

The day was dusty and windy and I feared that a sandstorm was brewing.

We were shown to seats. There were no seatbelts, and of

An Ilyushin Il-76 cargo plane.

course there was no what-to-do-in-the-case-of-an-emergency briefing. We chatted while the loadmaster fastened down the cargo and the pilot and crew went through the pre-flight checks.

Once the loadmaster was finished he came over to the seating area and took out plastic cups and a bottle of vodka and poured stiff shots into each cup. Three of these cups went to the pilots, a toast was made, and all of them downed their drinks.

Neither Mauritz nor I are spirit drinkers but we decided maybe the vodka wasn't a bad idea.

'The vodka's not going to kill us, Neil,' he said. 'Cheers!'

We touched cups and knocked back the white firewater. 'No,' I replied, 'but we might die from a drunken pilot.'

Takeoff went well and we were quickly circling up to gain altitude out of Baghdad airspace.

All of a sudden there was shouting in the cockpit. I could see the radio operator gesticulating madly. The plane made a drastic course change and then things quietened down. I was keen for another vodka at that point.

It seems we had had a near miss with a DHL cargo plane. In fact, to our guys watching from the airport it looked very much as if we were going to collide, as they came right out of the cloud cover next to us.

Eventually, hitching rides on cargo planes was stopped and we had to go through normal passport controls. The cargo flights were always interesting but I didn't exactly miss them.

22
Going high-profile

Although our preferred means of operating was low-profile, our clients would from time to time call for the high-profile approach.

On one occasion I was helping the team take guys who were headed back home on leave to the airport. We left at nine in the morning, which gave us plenty of time. There'd been a number of IEDs found along the airport road in recent days so we had added an extra hour in case we got caught behind a US sweep team.

There was nothing worse than missing a flight home.

No, there was something worse. And that was sitting in the departure lounge watching a sandstorm blow in, knowing that the planes wouldn't depart until the visibility improved. This would normally mean missing the Dubai connection and having no way of contacting your family.

On this mission we had the guys in the Ford transit van and their luggage in the minibus. The minibus was the gunship.

We crossed the river, drove past the university, passed the Al Mansour turn-off when the traffic started to slow and eventually came to a stop.

The locals climbed out of their vehicles, as was their wont, and it was soon confirmed that there was an IED at the next bridge. The US sweepers were there and would destroy it so the delay would not be long. We'd overtaken a fuel truck about 300 metres back and, as I didn't want it pulling up next to us, I moved into the right-hand lane in order to stay well ahead of it. Fuel trucks were always targets for bombs.

A number of high-profile teams passed on the left using the median between the outgoing and the incoming expressways. Whenever I noticed one approaching I'd warn the minibus. These high-profile teams were a threat to us, as they didn't know we were a PSD team and if they saw weapons they would likely open fire.

I had no sooner finished talking, than there was a massive explosion and the van was pushed forward by the blast. The minibus rammed us from the rear and a huge ball of fire engulfed the scene. At first I thought the fuel truck had detonated but when the smoke cleared I saw that one of the high-profile PSD vehicles had been rammed by a car bomb. As mentioned earlier, in technical terms this is known as a VBIED.

The targeted vehicle was a Humvee (a civilian vehicle, not a military one) and both it and the VBIED were burning. By good fortune, the fuel truck had not exploded. If it had we would all have been toast. The other thing in our favour was that we were ahead of the problem. Within ten minutes we were moving again.

I'd hoped we would make it all the way to the airport but at the approach checkpoint we were stopped once more.

As usual the high-profile teams forced their way through, hooters blowing and trying to push us out of the way. But they got no further than the checkpoint, the military refusing to let them through. Eventually a number of them were parked on the right-hand side of the road: perfect targets to be ambushed by insurgents. They were trapped there with no way out.

This thought was still going through my mind when these teams were hammered by PKM machine gun and AK-47 fire.

One of Safenet's armoured F250 vehicles after hitting an improvised explosive device (IED).

This armoured vehicle was hit from the side.

A PKM can penetrate an armoured vehicle. If it was firing armour-piercing rounds they'd be whizzing through as if the metal were no thicker than a tin can.

My team wanted to leap out and return fire.

'Sit tight,' I ordered. 'This is not our fight. We've not been fired at.'

I knew that if we were drawn into the firefight many of us would die. Our vehicles were not armour-plated and there was no way that this would end well for us.

The guys obeyed, their weapons in their hands.

Watching the reaction of the high-profile teams was not edifying.

Men dived out of the vehicles, returning fire on the wrong side of the road. Others fell out and dropped their weapons or their ammunition. Those who got into firing position then realised their ammunition was still in the vehicle so they ran back to grab it.

It was a farce. A comedy of errors.

I realised once again that not all the PSD teams were of the same calibre of men or had been well trained.

The firefight lasted about five minutes until a number of military Humvees arrived and their firepower cleaned up the ambush. It was an impressive show of force, and the PSD teams were lucky they'd come to the rescue.

The contact was not without its casualties. That more people weren't injured was extraordinary. But some children who had been playing soccer in the ambush area were shot and had to be rushed to hospital in the Humvees. Not long after they left, the checkpoint opened and we could get our guys to the airport on time.

GOING HIGH-PROFILE

The debate between high-profile and low-profile PSD work had no end. I made no bones about my preference but sometimes I had to back down and accept the clients' wishes.

One such occasion involved an ECC contract. Normally we ran low-profile missions with them and they were happy with that arrangement. But the military couldn't really understand our approach and remained sceptical and attached to the high-profile operation as being the safest in the more risky areas.

One of our team leaders, Craig Roets, received a request from some engineering clients for a high-profile mission to Mosul. We didn't have vehicles for such a mission at that time but the engineers did. These were four, low-mileage, spacious Ford Excursions with 7.3-litre turbo diesel engines. They had extended fuel tanks and could do the return trip to Mosul on a single tank. In short, they were fitted with everything that a PSD team could want. Each vehicle had both VHF (very high frequency) and HF (high frequency) radios fitted with whip antennae. My only reservation was that our handsets were programmed to a different frequency, which meant if we had to leave the vehicle in an emergency we would not have communication with our clients in the vans. To resolve this, we fitted an extra radio in each vehicle.

My other concern was that four of these black monsters in a convoy was a recipe for disaster. I didn't think we'd make it there and back without encountering an IED. We'd be an obvious target.

The mission was planned for three days (with an extra day built in for emergencies): a day to get there; a day in Mosul while the engineers repaired a radio installation damaged in a missile attack; and a day to drive back.

It was a simple enough mission, except that the vehicles were not what we were used to nor was the high-profile element.

Craig and I spent time working on blocking tactics should we be intercepted by insurgents, and decided that he would travel with the main client in the front vehicle, with the rest of the clients in the second Excursion. Should we be attacked, the procedure was to drive through the kill zone. I was uneasy about this as the enemy had the freedom to shoot at will, knowing that there was little chance of any retaliation from the gunship at the back of the convoy.

As we didn't have uniforms – because of our low-profile preference, which meant that we dressed as civilians – we decided to wear similar shirts and pants with the body armour over our shirts. At least this would give us a semblance of a security unit.

The only reason we had agreed to the mission was in the hopes of securing a long-term contract with the engineers. They were trying to persuade the military to approve the contract, but the military's traditional thinking that high-profile was best was a difficult obstacle to overcome. If we could prove that we were versatile enough to execute both types of missions, we'd be in a better position to sign on the dotted line.

John didn't like the idea. He was not in favour of the high-profile approach. To him this was the Blackwater approach and he regarded them as a bunch of arrogant bodybuilders. In one memorable incident he'd almost come to blows with one of their team leaders after they'd tried to ram us off the road inside the airport precinct.

'It'll be all right,' I tried to reassure him. 'We all know low-profile is best but we've got no option here.'

'You just want to play Rambo like the rest of them,' he responded. 'You guys love being the heavies.'

It was clear he believed a high-profile monster raged inside me dying to get out. This wasn't true at all but I could see that I'd never convince him otherwise.

On departure day we found we'd be transporting more clients than anticipated. Most of them were military guys and the contracting officer for the security contract we were after. Our arrival caused some puzzlement because we pitched up at our clients' villa in the Green Zone in a minibus that looked like an ordinary taxi.

'You've just come from the Red Zone in that!' the contracting officer said to me, pointing at our vehicle. 'Is it armoured?'

I told him it wasn't. But we'd put plates on the inside to give us some protection.

'Why've you got red taxi number plates?'

'Because it's registered with the Iraqi traffic authority as a taxi.'

'Really!' He was clearly astonished.

'This bus comes from Erbil,' I explained. 'But mostly we buy our vehicles in Sadr City.'

No Americans in their right minds would venture into Sadr City. It was not just in the Red Zone; it was so alien and dangerous to them it might as well have been another planet.

I explained to him how we bought number plates and had them transferred to OSSI/Safenet. Number plates were never destroyed but passed from one owner to the next.

'Hell, man, you're crazy,' he said, shaking his head. 'I've never heard anything like this before.' It was too much for him and I should probably have spared him the detail.

Craig now gave the clients a briefing of the route and how

we'd be proceeding and I heard the contracting officer saying to one of his colleagues, 'These guys know their stuff. Never been to a briefing like this.'

In the end we set off with only the four clients. The contracting officer shook my hand. 'You guys do some strange things but you're obviously not gung-ho types.'

I took up my seat in the gunship and we left the compound in typical Blackwater fashion, bumper to bumper. John would have been thoroughly annoyed.

At the exit gate I expected to be stopped, but with these vehicles and their military registrations we were waved straight through. It was a new and strange experience for me.

The Excursions had huge power, and the acceleration pushed you back into the seat. On Route Irish we were soon up to 120 km/h. This, too, was a strange experience for me. I'd never driven at this speed inside Baghdad. Another oddity was watching civilian vehicles get out of the way or slow down radically if they thought they were getting too close to our convoy. These four monsters must have been a terrifying sight to them.

It didn't take long before we were on the road to Mosul. I had never had such an easy transit through town. The first checkpoint had waved us through the military lane and we had not even slowed down. This was also something I wasn't used to. Normally we'd spend at least half an hour at a checkpoint, often longer. This was a serious plus for the high-profile teams. No wonder they were irritated when traffic held them up.

The drive up to Mosul went like clockwork even though I expected an IED at any and every moment. I was sure an informant would phone ahead to have his insurgent compatriots arrange an ambush. But this didn't happen.

Instead we were soon settled on the US base with great rooms and a good dining facility.

'Listen, guys,' I said to the engineers. 'If you're inclined to stay longer, that's no problem with us.'

Of course we were not that lucky. The engineers completed their work in a day, and on day three we headed back to Baghdad, leaving early in the morning. Again all went without incident until we arrived at the checkpoint outside Baghdad where the traffic was backed up for kilometres.

No problem. The Excursions had a high clearance so we climbed the kerb into the oncoming traffic. And then, hazards and lights on, we roared contraflow down the lane with vehicles pulling over to let us pass. We even went through the checkpoint on the wrong side without the military raising any objections. They probably thought we were a US military PSD team with a high-ranking officer on board.

In no time at all we were back in the Green Zone, our clients safe and sound in their villa. I couldn't believe that we'd accomplished the mission without incident.

'It was a great mission,' I told John. 'Nothing better than sailing through the checkpoints.'

'So you guys think that's the way to do it now?' he said.

'Have to admit it's got its advantages.'

I think he was rather disappointed that, we hadn't encountered any trouble. But I have to admit that, those advantages aside, I couldn't have lived with the daily knowledge that I was an IED magnet. It would have driven me to distraction knowing that I had to rely on the vehicle for my protection. All told, that mission confirmed my preference for low-profile missions.

The irony of ironies was that we didn't get the contract, as

John refused to accept the clause that we would have to do high-profile missions when requested. At that stage we had more than enough work and John didn't want the other clients to realise that they could choose to be protected by high-profile teams.

Some of the high-profile team members of Safenet in front of one of their armoured F250 vehicles.

In later years Mauritz would start the high-profile teams for ECC. This was the beginning of the end of the OSSI/Safenet joint company.

I have to say that I had huge respect for the high-profile guys. They were targets wherever they went and had to rely on their skill and the protection their vehicles provided. It takes a certain type of hard-core guy to be able to work under these conditions. Every time you climb into the vehicle you don't know if you'll climb out. Some days they could hit three IEDs in the space of a couple of hours. Luckily, not all the IEDs were direct hits and usually the guys escaped with minor injuries.

Low-profile had its hazards and you had to fit in where you were most comfortable. My feeling was that low-profile guys could work the high-profile approach but that this seldom worked the other way round. Habits acquired as a high-profile operator were hard to unlearn. In high-profile everything was focused on the vehicle; in low-profile everything was about your disguise.

23

The Baghdad Four continued

The kidnapping of our four South African men – André Durant, Johann Enslin, Callie Scheepers and Hardus Greeff – had a major impact on our company. We had never experienced anything like it. For a company that had been through the mill and lost only one operative, the capture of these men was devastating.

I had evaluated and trained the four when they first started out. While I didn't know them very well on a personal level they were well liked by the rest of the team.

As I was part of the management team at the time, I know how the mission was planned and how the incident unfolded. The mission came about because our client, ECC, needed to get critical supplies and electronic equipment to Kirkush, a forward operating base near the border with Iran. A number of attempts had been made using high-profile teams from other companies and all had failed. As time went on, the need for the equipment became increasingly urgent and ECC decided to use a low-profile team to escort the truck with the equipment to the site.

This was were we came in.

The mission date was set for 10 December 2006, with André as the team leader. As planned, the team left the villa early that Sunday morning. At this stage the convoy comprised three vehicles: a soft-skin Nissan Patrol, an armoured vehicle and a minibus acting as gunship. The intention was to collect the truck where it had been parked overnight at a power station. This was a plant where OSSI/Safenet provided security.

THE BAGHDAD FOUR CONTINUED

In André's armoured vehicle was a tracker unit. This unit was linked to our ops room and to the US operations room. If André triggered the tracker unit it emitted a silent panic alarm that would activate an alarm in both ops rooms. At that point incident management plans would immediately be operational.

Team leaders knew they were to activate the alarm in any circumstances where they thought that the team was threatened by any force or incident. This meant either an attack on the convoy or the detonation of an IED. The unit was plugged into the vehicle's cigarette lighter, so it needed power to work.

As I have shown, it was not common practice for low-profile teams to escort convoys. The low-profile advantage was its disguise. In this instance the moment the cargo truck joined the convoy the low-profile aspect would be compromised and the convoy would be a target.

The team had almost cleared Baghdad when the tracker monitor showed that they had been stationary for a while. This was not red-flagged as the team was close to the Iraqi checkpoint at the entrance to Baghdad. Also, it was early morning and the traffic was heavy. It was presumed that the electronic pings from the tracker unit had been delayed and that this was the reason for the team's stationary position.

Then the ops room received a call from one of our Iraqi team members who wanted to confirm that one of our teams was escorting a truck out of Baghdad.

He was told this was correct.

'They have been stopped at a fake checkpoint,' he said. 'Tell them to get out of there as quickly as they can.'

An urgent message was sent to André that they had entered a fake checkpoint, but the ops room couldn't get through to him or any of the other team members.

Our local man, who had stopped close by, then gave the ops officer a running account of what was taking place before his eyes. He had been on his way to work when he saw the team on the other side of the road. When he realised what was going on he stopped a discreet distance away. He described the men getting out of the vehicles, handing over their weapons, taking off their body armour. He confirmed that a man dressed in a police uniform had gone to the armoured vehicle and removed the tracker.

Two of the Iraqis, who were part of the mission and also abducted that day, would later tell us that the policemen manning the checkpoint had convinced André that they were looking for PSD vehicles that had been identified as car bombs. They claimed that one of our vehicles fitted the description of the suspected VBIED and that was why they needed to search the vehicle and all the equipment.

The team complied, since they were under the impression it was a legitimate checkpoint. According to our Iraqi witness, as soon as all the team members were outside the vehicles they were arrested and loaded into police vehicles.

The minibus gunship had fallen behind and wasn't at the checkpoint when the first two vehicles were stopped. When they came close enough to the checkpoint and realised what was happening, they tried to turn around but they were blocked by a police vehicle that forced them to move to the checkpoint. Clearly these policemen were in cahoots with those manning the checkpoint.

At this point our duty officer contacted the US ops room and told them our team had been captured at a fake checkpoint. The Americans immediately scrambled the reaction force while our local man followed the hostage takers to a police station, but he then panicked when he thought he was compromised.

I was standing in our ops room listening to all this with horror and disbelief. This was our worst nightmare.

'Keep me posted,' I shouted to the ops manager and headed downstairs to get a taxi to our headquarters.

Things now went a little crazy.

We placed a PSD team on high alert so that they could be dispatched to the scene immediately if we received any useful information from the Americans, or if André's team contacted our ops room. Additional guys with weapons and ammunition were added to the team in case the situation demanded that sort of firepower.

There was heated debate as to what should be done. I was all for going to find our guys straight away. We knew where they had last been seen. I was sure that they could not have been taken far from the fake checkpoint. We had enough trained guys to mount an extraction operation in any situation. Of course, there was always the possibility of casualties in such an eventuality, but I reckoned that if I asked for volunteers they would all step forward. Being taken hostage was the worst thing that could happen to anybody.

On the other hand, there was an insurgent military force in Sadr City, close to where the abduction took place, and there was no way that nine or ten guys would be able to take them on. We would most likely all be killed.

Furthermore, the majority of the members on the management team were against any offensive action and there was good reason for this. And in hindsight this was probably the right approach. We were not at war. We were only a security company and could not justify direct action. It would have been illegal.

We had done what we could: we had notified the military,

there were patrols in the area looking for our guys. But that still left us feeling impotent.

I contacted Mauritz and John. They were both stunned.

'We've got the kidnap and hostage policy,' said Mauritz. 'You better notify the insurers in case we need it.'

We paid a lot of money each year to have this policy, and it covered a ransom demand as well as the costs of a hostage negotiator. Within days of notification, a hostage negotiator arrived in Baghdad. (He would remain in the city for many months in case the kidnappers made contact.)

But until then we were glued to our radio for updates by the US patrols. Their reports came in regularly as they searched the area. All to no avail.

By now the security companies had all been informed and were also on the lookout for our missing guys. With each hour that passed I thought the chances of finding them decreased. By the next day I reckoned we'd be lucky if we found them alive.

At this point there had still been no ransom demand or any contact from the kidnappers.

On Tuesday 12 December we received word that the locals from the team had been released and dropped off at different locations. They'd been told that if they contacted us they and their families would be killed. We tried to contact them but they refused (understandably) to answer their phones.

Later we exerted renewed pressure on the men to give us more information. Eventually two of them met with us secretly. Three of them left for Syria shortly after the incident and were never heard from again. The two men told us that initially the checkpoint had looked genuine. Everyone wore uniforms, the vehicles all looked official.

Once our guys had opened the doors of the armoured

vehicle things had quickly gone bad. With the demands for the weapons and body armour came the realisation that they were in serious trouble. They were then blindfolded and driven away. At one point the vehicles had stopped and there'd been shouting. Apparently the kidnappers hadn't expected expats. They were simply after the truck.

They told us that the locals had been held in a different location to the expats. On the day of their release, the locals said they heard a guard being shouted at for not keeping blindfolds on the expats. They'd been told by one of the guards that the expats would soon be released. In the meantime they were not to say anything to the security company.

Both of the men we interviewed – and we interviewed them separately – told the same story with only minor differences in the order of events.

We became increasingly worried. Meetings were held with local leaders to see if we could make contact with any groups that might have kidnapped our guys. We sent one man to Iran to see if a group there had been responsible for the incident. Days went by. There were no leads, no ransom requests.

There was a constant stream of informers offering information for money, but when we demanded proof they quietly disappeared.

The insurance company also worked whatever angles and contacts they had but they too came up empty-handed.

On 21 December we heard that André Durant had made a short call to his wife confirming that they were alive and being looked after. 'Don't stop praying for us,' were his last words before the line went dead.[1]

This call gave us hope that they'd be released soon. Maybe the PSD locals had been right.

More days passed. Nothing happened. We heard nothing. Again the black concern descended. If they were going to be released it would have happened already.

I suspected that our guys had been killed, as they would be able to identify the police officials involved. I believed that the uniforms were genuine and that these were policemen conducting business on the side.

Two months later, during February, an operation was launched in Sadr City, and if they'd been held there they would surely have been found. This didn't happen.

There have been many rumours regarding the missing Baghdad Four over the years. There were rumours that we did not want to pay ransom, yet I know that a ransom would have been paid if there was proof of life. But no ransom demand was ever received. Certainly not while I was with OSSI/Safenet.

Many years later, in Najaf in 2015, I learnt that a captured terrorist had claimed that he was involved in the murder of the four South Africans. I was never able to confirm this and put it down to just another wild story. The men were officially declared dead in 2011.

---

[1] Otto, H. "Vroue verklaar hul mans dood," in *Beeld*, 15 October 2011. See http://152.111.1.88/argief/berigte/beeld/2011/10/15/B1/8/thoBagdadSCOOP.html, accessed 5 January 2018.

24

The end of OSSI/Safenet

Throughout this book I have tried to show the reality of PSD work in Iraq. It was not glamorous or exciting. Just driving to the airport to drop or pick up clients was a risk. You could be involved in an IED detonation or an attack by insurgents, or rammed by a car bomb, and you need not necessarily be the target. You could be collateral damage.

PSD work was always stressful and fraught with the possibility of danger. We lost five men during my time with OSSI/Safenet and that was not a small price to pay for our efforts to safeguard the lives of others in that violent country. Others among my colleagues sustained wounds from some of our close encounters. Others bear emotional and psychological scars from the trauma they saw that will haunt them for the rest of their lives.

However, I regard our record as a remarkable achievement that can only be attributed to the quality of the South Africans who worked for us. Also our low-profile manner was highly successful and effective. We literally wrote the manual for low-profile PSD missions, which contained training instructions and operational procedures gained from experience and feedback from the guys in the field conducting missions.

The other thing about PSD work was the tedium. On most of our missions – despite the possibility of danger – we were nothing more than a taxi service. We would drive the client to some location and then sit around for hours, or days, waiting for them to finish their work.

And then there were the off days. Okay, you weren't on duty but what were you going to do with yourself for those long hours until the next mission? In the Green Zone there was the pool and the gym but out on the remote sites there was nothing. On top of that you couldn't always look forward to the next meal as the food was not that exciting.

With slow internet – or often no internet at all – entertainment was in short supply. Some of the sites had basic gym equipment and this was the only distraction we had. But even here the guys needed to be monitored. Most of them imbibed energy shakes, but some of them moved on to pills and steroid injections. Often these drugs brought with them a personality change, and men would become aggressive. A few had to be fired for this very reason. In some of the American security companies part of the medical included a drug test for steroids, and they were strict about enforcing a no-drug rule.

One of the things about low-profile work was that you needed men who were stable and not drug addicts, or the whole team could be at risk.

Aside from that, you had to monitor everyone's psychological make-up. Some drivers were inclined to road rage, some of our staff had racist issues working with locals. In fact this latter attitude was a sure sign that something was wrong.

Some wives thought their husbands were out there having fun all the time. But after three months of tension and boredom no one would be having much fun any more. That 28-day leave break was a much-needed time of recuperation.

Most guys doing this work did it because it was the only sort of work they knew and for the money. It was a way of putting bread on the table. But being a security officer in a far-off country and keeping a family at home halfway happy was impossible for many. Most of the guys that I worked with ended up divorced. Many of them went through two or three marriages. I could count on one hand the guys still married to their first wives. My feeling is there were two reasons for this strain on the marriage: the one was the long periods away from home; the other was financial. Money gave the men the freedom to look around. Okay, maybe their wives were also to blame, maybe there was a cocktail of reasons for the failure of these marriages. But one thing is for sure: marriage bust-ups were one of the tragedies of this line of work.

Furthermore, guys all responded differently to the daily routine, which is what made managing this sort of company so challenging. On top of that came the demands of clients, which could often put themselves and the teams in danger. There were many times when I would have to disagree with a client and often there would be a stalemate for a few hours. Fortunately, in most occasions my rationale prevailed.

And then there was the business of managing our personnel. Managing so many guys running missions in so many different directions was challenging, especially in a country where identity documents were essential. From your passport to your badges to get you through the checkpoints, you needed to have your identity paperwork on hand. One of my greatest fears was that a passport would go missing. Bureaucracy was not something you wanted to test in a country such as Iraq at that time.

Naturally this thing I dreaded eventually happened.

The guilty party was one Wayne Crumm. He'd had his passport in his pouch in the morning but when he returned from the mission it was gone. He was going on leave shortly and for that a passport was essential. I had visions of his having to phone home to tell his wife he'd lost his passport. What wife would believe such a story?

Replacing a passport could only be done in Jordan, the nearest South African consulate. However, on a flight from Dubai to Amman I'd had a stroke of luck and had met one of the women who worked in the South African embassy. She'd said she was ready to help if I had problems. Little did either of us know that I'd be contacting her so soon.

'You're going to have to get him to Jordan,' she said. 'Give me his flight details and I'll meet him at the airport with an emergency passport.'

I emailed a photo of Wayne and all his details to her.

The next problem was getting Wayne through passport control at Baghdad. The ever-resourceful Hassan came to my assistance and produced a lawyer who had a contact at the airport. For $500 he could get Wayne through the checkpoint. It meant relying on people I didn't know, but what other option was there? All went according to plan and later that afternoon Wayne was back at Villa T-Bone with a temporary passport.

There were incidents like this all the time. Minor matters which had the potential to make life very difficult. Afterwards, however, we would all enjoy a good laugh.

When I look back at my time, from our early naive days of setting up the business, I am amazed at the professionalism of the organisation we came to manage. Without Rieme and Snoeks and Eddie and our local man Hassan, it would have been difficult getting OSSI/Safenet up and running. They were resourceful and diligent men with great stamina for the job. Of course, it was not all hard work; we had our laughs, our quiet moments, and those Friday braais that became an institution were a lifesaver. Undoubtedly there were good times. There are always good times even in the worst of times.

There'd been a tension between Mauritz and John from the beginning. As the months and years went by, their relationship deteriorated. When Mauritz bought out the ECC contract, the writing was on the wall that the company would eventually split.

As had often been the case, I was caught in the middle. Eventually, at the end of 2006, I decided to call it quits. In 2007 I explored new opportunities in Afghanistan but they didn't turn out as I had hoped. By then Vivienne, who is a trained ICU nurse, was on a three-year contract at one of the international hospitals in Abu Dhabi, and I joined her there in December 2007.

It's the story of my life; I was no sooner in Abu Dhabi than I got a call from John.

'I've heard that you're at a loose end, Neil,' he said. 'How about coming to work for OSSI? I need a manager. I've tried some guys but none of them know how to run a security company. You've got the insight.'

I was tempted.

'I don't mind Mauritz having ECC, I'm happy with the contracts I have. I'm making money, but I need help. Also I don't want to put in a lot of effort and make Mauritz money at my expense.'

'Okay,' I said on the spur of the moment. 'I'll come through to Baghdad.'

Being back in Baghdad was weird. The guys welcomed me, but were suspicious that I was working with the 'enemy'. This made me the 'enemy' as well.

Because I'd set up the company, I knew intimately how it operated and nobody could hide anything from me. I decided that if I had to keep tabs on John's interests my best bet was to move into the team villa in the Green Zone. That would give me free access to the clients and I would not be dependent on Safenet to drive me around or lend me a car. John had a loyal bunch of guys working for him, and Safenet had very little to do with the running of this side of the business. They did, however, maintain the vehicles, and we had to rely on them for all the personal administration, including badging, salaries and flights.

To me, being totally reliant on the goodwill of Safenet wasn't a good situation. If they decided to pull the plug on OSSI, we wouldn't have a leg to stand on and would lose all the contracts we were currently running.

'This is not an ideal situation,' I told John. 'The best thing we can do is get a security licence.'

'That's going to be damn difficult,' he replied. 'For a foreign company to get a licence these days is almost impossible.'

'Yeah, but what if we went in as a local company?' I said.

John had employed a guy called Ali Al-Hassona in 2005. Ali was from a rich Iraqi family who had lived abroad during Saddam's reign. His father was in the garment trade and Ali had been schooled in England and Italy – to all intents and purposes he had been brought up in Western culture. He spoke English with a British accent. He spoke fluent Arabic, too, but nobody was ever the wiser – the locals never realised that he was an Iraqi.

At the time, we decided that Ali would be a great asset as an undercover expat. He could listen in on conversations between Iraqis without them knowing he understood Arabic.

END OF OSSI/SAFENET

We introduced him to the other expats as a Brit who'd been a pro basketball player in Oman, which was almost all true.

His highly religious family claimed a direct bloodline to the prophet Muhammad. I suspect they hoped that he would one day follow this calling.

'Why don't we use Ali to get a licence,' I suggested to John. 'With his family connections it shouldn't be too difficult. All you've got to do is negotiate a deal with Ali and set up the company accordingly.'

This they did, and soon the licence process was under way. I pushed Ali to hurry the process as I was worried that Safenet would get wind of what we were doing and our relationship with them would sour. I knew the last thing they would expect was for us to acquire a licence. Going in as a local company made a lot of sense, as it bypassed much of the red tape, from the Ministry of Trade licence to accounting documentation.

I reckoned it would take a month for the licence to come through, fully expecting that Safenet could pull out of the company at any moment.

We duly got our licence, and then the negotiations to split OSSI from Safenet started in 2007. Knowing the animosity between John and Mauritz, and that they would not be able to come to an arrangement that was the best for both companies and the clients, I suggested that Gerhard and I come to an agreement and then convince our principals.

We sat down to do this. The biggest issues were around dividing the vehicles, weapons and signal equipment, including the trackers, but eventually we had an agreement. I reckoned that the only reason Gerhard was amenable was because he did not know that we had a security licence. I guess they underestimated us.

By the time this agreement was in place we had set up a

payroll for our expats and for our locals, which ensured that their work would continue if Mauritz wiped them off his payroll. In fact we got all our paperwork in order so that, when the moment came, our PSD teams would have the requisite identity documents, social security and the right badging. I needed to ensure a smooth transition to the new company. As I expected, once we signed the agreement, Safenet stopped paying our staff. No problem. We picked up the tab and only then did they realise that we had gone our own way. We even put new stickers on the PSD vehicles. The final round came when Safenet sent our clients new contracts – we merely intercepted them and showed our bona fides and convinced our clients that we were legal and legitimate.

Safenet unfortunately ran into problems at this point. The contracts with ECC ended and were not renewed, as the Americans decided to withdraw from Iraq. The accounting company that had handled their social security, and was supposed to pay the monthly amount, reneged and only paid some of the monies due. This meant that locals who left the company found they would not be paid their social security contributions. This was a major issue for Safenet and eventually led to their decision to leave the country. That made things easier for us, as they were forced to get rid of their equipment.

My time in Iraq continued through the decade, and I remained with OSSI as the country manager in Iraq and later Afghanistan. It was a time of violence and danger but also of camaraderie and laughter. And, yes, the salary was good, but the cost for many of my colleagues was in their lives and in their personal relationships.

I have no idea why some people think it is glamourous to be involved in a conflict area. That is the last thing it is. Most of the time, it's a struggle to keep the mind occupied and the family half happy. Sadly there were a number of deaths, but there were even more divorces as families were sacrificed for the time we spent in Iraq. This may have been the biggest tragedy of the private security industry in Iraq.

There were many who should never have gone to Iraq for this reason. There were others who did not have the training or the military and operational background for the missions we had to run. I went because I knew I was good at that kind of work. I would have loved to spend my time with my wife and been able to watch my sons grow up. I would have preferred that to being in the desert.

But I needed to earn a living to cater for their needs and wants. They understood this, and they understood that their comforts were dependent on my line of work. Had I remained in the SANDF we would never have enjoyed the standard of living we had.

After Iraq and Afghanistan came spells in Haiti and Libya until, in 2013, I finally left OSSI and went to work for Triple Canopy as a project manager back in Iraq, this time in the oilfields. That job lasted until 2016 when, still in Iraq, I moved to a Korean company called Shield, as their country manager.

Nowadays I'm freelance. As the Bob Dylan song has it, 'blowin' in the wind'.

Postscript

Of the people I worked with during that initial stint in Iraq, **John Walbridge** has handed control of OSSI over to his two sons although, in his retirement, he still retains an active interest in the security industry. His sons were initially in finance in the US but with the move to security set up the company in Afghanistan. John has been much less hands-on since 2013 but due to his vast network will probably never retire completely as he remains constantly on the look-out for new and interesting opportunities. As he puts it, he doesn't want to do the heavy lifting any more but likes being involved. OSSI has operational interests in Iraq in the oil industry, Afghanistan, Haiti and Libya.

When Safenet left Iraq, **Mauritz le Roux** put his energies into the South African side of the company. He then had an opportunity to buy into a company that was operating in Iraq. This company, SSSI, had been started by one of the men Mauritz had sent to Afghanistan to investigate the possibility of starting Safenet in that country. Mauritz jumped at the opportunity and rehired most of the team that he had used in Iraq. He was also able to activate contacts with the construction company ECCI because they had moved to Afghanistan to undertake road construction projects. Mauritz later also got involved in Angola with a training programme for that country's government. He bought a house in Cape Town and with his sons opened a brewery. Mauritz, as always, is still looking for opportunities in the Middle East and makes regular trips to Iraq and other countries.

POSTSCRIPT

Since those now distant days, **Rieme de Jager** has been involved in a number of different projects, not all of them security-related and not all of them in Iraq. Due to his extensive African network, he specialises in projects on this continent. We remain in annual contact but he is a taciturn guy and seldom has much to say about his current projects. He is one of the first guys I would take with me on any difficult task as I have a huge respect for his abilities.

Snoeks Niewhoud moved with Mauritz from Iraq to Afghanistan. He and I were colleagues and respected one another's expertise in the security industry but were never close friends. With his move to Kurdistan we lost contact, but I have kept abreast of his movements through Mauritz. He has always worked in the security business and is still involved. I'd heard that he bought a house in Mozambique close to one of the better diving spots in the southern parts of the country. He was always an avid diver. As far as I know he still lives in KwaZulu-Natal.

I have stayed in contact with **Eddie Visser** over the years and in writing this book he supplied me with the photographs of the early days. I have always had great respect for Eddie and admired his passion for his profession. He has been a great ambassador. Eddie was newly married when we left for Iraq. Once he decided his tour of duty was over there, he returned home to start a family. Since then he's had three children. On the work front he soon became involved in establishing remote clinics (recruiting staff and training them) for companies operating in isolated and hostile places. This took him to Sierra Leone, Benin, Nigeria, the Democratic Republic of Congo, Uganda, Madagascar, China and Papua New Guinea. Currently he consults for endovascular surgeons. A passionate mountain biker, Eddie has participated in many such events in South Africa.

In 2008 it became too dangerous for **Hassan Salam** to safely live in Iraq. He and his family had received death threats and it reached a stage where Mauritz decided that Hassan should be moved to the Dubai office of Safenet. Hassan made the move but eventually left the company and went to work for a construction company owned by a relation in Dubai. He married an Iraqi woman and they have a son. Hassan then applied for an American visa and this was granted and he and his family moved to the United States. I still have occasional contact with him and always revert to him if I need to find a reliable person in Iraq.

Sitting here at my computer, reading what I have written, I have to ask myself: why? Why did I take the chances I did, first in the South African Defence Force and later in the private security industry? Why did I follow the path that I did? After all, there are safer ways to make a living, employment that would not see me end up in jail in a foreign country for breaking some stupid law or be killed by some warlord or gun-runner that I had pissed off.

I wasn't in it for the money, because I was not making the big money. That went to my employers. The only answer that I can honestly give is that working as a private military contractor offered the kick I so desperately needed to give meaning to my life, to make me happy. I lived off the adrenaline.

This was what all those years in the bush during the Border War left me with – the sense that this feeling was normal and the constant need to push the envelope in everything I did. I never accepted that something could not be done because the risks were too high.

POSTSCRIPT

Many who served in the Border War were left with psychological scars, and this was mine. It came down to a kind of self-destruct mode, and the game was to beat the destruct. I think this was one of the underlying reasons why I decided to write about my experiences. It is a way of closing the book and finding myself again.

Writing this book has offered a way to look at life differently. Now I can see the beautiful things around me that I could not see in the past – the beautiful wife and children that the Lord has blessed me with, the grandchildren I have today. Now is the time to enjoy the important things in life that I neglected when I was chasing the self-destruct. I think that I have finally learned how to live and to love again and to cherish life and all the blessings it brings.

If you take the time to stop and really look, you will see life in all its glory. Too many of our generation never stopped to look and appreciate, and life passed them by. They never found the peace and the beauty that life has to offer. If there is one thought I would like to leave you with as the reader, it is to make sure you stop often enough to look at and see life.

www.ingramcontent.com/pod-product-compliance
Lightning Source LLC
Chambersburg PA
CBHW070840160426
43192CB00012B/2254